Political Risk Assessment: Concept, Method, and Management

A Reader
To Accompany

*The Handbook of Country
and
Political Risk Analysis*

Llewellyn D. Howell, Ph.D.
Editor

Published by
The PRS Group, Inc.
6320 Fly Road, Suite 102, P.O. Box 248
East Syracuse, NY 13057-0248 USA
Tel: +1 (315) 431-0511 • Fax: +1 (315) 431-0200
www.prsgroup.com ~ www.countrydata.com

© The PRS Group, Inc., 2001
Political Risk Assessment: Concept, Method, and Management
ISBN: 1-931077-13-4

Printed in U.S.A.
Manufactured by Dupli Envelope & Graphics Corporation

Political Risk Assessment: Concept, Method, and Management

Table of Contents

Preface

This edition of *Political Risk Assessment: Concept, Method, and Management* was designed to accompany the methodological text *The Handbook of Country and Political Risk Analysis*, now in its third edition (2001). *The Handbook* is a compilation of methodologies that are employed by major service corporations, financial institutions, and industries to assess country and political risk as guidance for foreign investors. Apart from a methodological introduction and an appended case, *The Handbook* is a descriptive presentation of systems by which country ratings are derived.

Political Risk Assessment takes another approach. It is, first of all, focused on political risk as distinct from the broader country risk. It is also primarily evaluative, with discussion of the concept, of developments in the field of political risk, of research on political risk issues, and, especially, of management of the risk that is detailed by the methods in *The Handbook*. The authors are practitioners who have a great depth of experience in the field of political risk analysis and work with firms active in international investment. The work presented calls for comment and responses from readers should be directed to the Editor at The PRS Group. The collective body of writings seeks to stimulate discussion that will hopefully be captured in subsequent publications.

The initial organization for this set of presentations came at a conference at Thunderbird, The American Graduate School of International Management. The conference was co-sponsored by Thunderbird's International Trade & Finance Center (ITFC) and The PRS Group and was entitled "Country and Political Risk Analysis: Models, Methods, and Management." It was held in Glendale, Arizona, April 29-30, 1999. Among the authors in this compendium, the following were presenters at that conference and provided initial versions of the chapters included here: Sandy Markwick, Walter Molano, Roger Shields, Gerald West, and Llewellyn Howell. I would like to express my appreciation to Dr. John Mathis of ITFC/Thunderbird for his contribution as co-organizer of the conference, for bringing together this distinguished group of practitioner scholars.

I would also like to thank Suzy Howell, Managing Editor of the *Thunderbird International Business Review* for her extensive assistance in handling correspondence and especially editing for this book. A tremendous number of hours has gone into bringing together these works from authors now spread around the globe. Also due thanks is Toni Siragusa who was instrumental in compiling the bibliography appended to the book. And lastly, my appreciation to Mary Lou Walsh of The PRS Group for both her editing efforts and her patience during the many months that it took to bring this publication to fruition.

This is obviously not the final word on political risk assessment but is instead what I hope will be a continuing discussion on what is an increasingly important field. Let us hear from you.

Llewellyn D. Howell
Editor
April 2001

About the Authors

C.W.J. Bradley is Managing Director at DBA Risk Management, Ltd., based in London, England.

William Dugan is Director of Operations and Senior Editor of Emerging Market Political Risk Reports for Summit Analytical Associates in Manchester, NH.

Llewellyn D. Howell is Professor of International Management at Thunderbird, The American Graduate School of International Management, in Glendale, AZ.

Sandy Markwick is a political risk consultant and former Senior Latin American Analyst at Control Risks Group (CRG) based in London, England.

Keith Martin is a Policy and Research Officer in the Policy and Evaluations Department of the Multilateral Investment Guarantee Agency (MIGA), a member of the World Bank Group, in Washington, DC.

Walter Molano is a Senior Managing Director and Head of Economic and Financial Research for BCP securities, in Greenwich, CT.

Michael K. O'Leary is Professor Emeritus at Syracuse University and Director of *Political Risk Services*, publications of The PRS Group, Inc., and he is based in London, England.

Roger E. Shields is President of Shields and Associates in Shorthills, NJ.

Daniel Wagner is Regional Manager of Southeast Asia Political Risks with the American International Group (AIG) and is based in Singapore.

Gerald T. West is Manager, Operations Evaluation, at the Multilateral Investment Guarantee Agency (MIGA), a member of the World Bank Group, in Washington, DC.

Chapter 1

Defining and Operationalizing Political Risk
Llewellyn D. Howell

What is Political Risk?

In today's globalized economic and business system, political risk assessment and management are increasingly more critical aspects of foreign direct investment. Especially as private investment replaces foreign aid that was a byproduct of competition between superpowers, understanding the relationship between politics and economics has become an integral part of simple national and planetary survival. This is an even more vital task as we enter a new millennium and find that commodities, services, and investment cross borders more freely than ever. Many have written of "political risk" for foreign investors since the 1960s, but both the calculation and the utilization of risk forecasts have been widely varied in the effort to bring this information to bear in international business. In this chapter I will bring together some of these concepts and applications in an effort to make the concept of political risk clearer in an application and management context. That is, I will define the term but also show ways that it can be operationalized such that it can be become a regular business tool for international investors.

The classic definition of political risk relates to the role and actions of national governments.

> Political risks are associated with government actions which deny or restrict the right of an investor/owner: (1) to use or benefit from his/her assets; or (2) which reduce the value of a firm. The most well known of the political risks include: war, revolutions, government seizure of property (expropriation, nationalization, or confiscation), and actions to restrict the movement of profits or other revenues from within a country.... Political risks are those associated with acts of government, whereas commercial

risk includes insolvency of a buyer or other economic reasons for nonpayment.[1]

Under this national level definition, the loss types include: 1) Confiscation; 2) Contract repudiation; 3) Currency inconvertibility; 4) Discriminatory taxation; 5) Embargo; 6) Expropriation of property; 7) Nationalization; 8) War risk; and 9) Wrongful calling of guarantees. While each of these is a genuine loss that is sourced in the government of a country, there are three reasons to expand the list.

The first is that this list is limited to those acts that can be insured (i.e. they are the non-commercial losses). There are many acts by governments, such as operations interference with the imposition of affirmative action hiring quotas, which are not insurable. Corrupt governments often demand bribes or employment for relatives or friends, a politically based cost to the investor that is not recoverable through insurance.

The second is that many acts in the political domain, which can result in losses, do not emanate from the government. In war risk, for example, rebellion against the government is counted even though it may not be a government choice. But civil strife and even civil war can arise (and does these days) between ethnic groups in a country where the government is simply a bystander or even powerless to intervene if it wanted to. Such incidents are covered by political risk insurance from the Overseas Private Investment Corporation (OPIC) of the U.S. government or the Multilateral Investment Guarantee Agency (MIGA) of the World Bank, even though no particular fault lies with the official national government. Control is the issue rather than formal structures or institutions. Direct attacks by guerrilla groups on foreign investors results in losses that don't originate with the country's government nor do they necessarily have anything to do with the government *per se*, although their efforts may be directed *at* the government. Racial, religious, and cultural groups are fragmenting in the new global order at a faster pace than many governments can accommodate.

The third reason is that national governments are not always the authoritative source of loss problems. Increasingly regional, provincial, state, and local (including tribal) governments are involved in dealing with investors in ways that national

---

[1] John O'Connell, "Political Risk," in John J. O'Connell, ed., *Blackwell Encyclopedic Dictionary of International Management*, Cambridge, MA: Blackwell Publishers, Ltd., 1997, p. 230-232.

governments don't and can't know about. In Vietnam there have been instances of city governments expropriating foreign businesses with the national government unable by its nature to even keep track of what all of its sub-units are doing.

Janice Monti-Belkaoui and Ahmed Riahi-Belkaoui have examined the wide range of attempts at operationalization of political risk and find that there is no real consensus.[2] Some researchers (and presumably managers) stick with a strict government decision and action definition, while others range to a complete "environment" explanation. International business texts provide their own varying views. Punnett and Ricks define political risk as "the possibility of unwanted consequences of political activity.... Companies face three major categories of political risk as follows: forced divestiture, unwelcome regulation, and interference with operations."[3] This is similar to the classic definition focused on government actions. Griffin and Pustay look at political risk as "any changes in the political environment that may adversely affect the value of the firm's business activities."[4] They include operating risk, which is a threat to ongoing operations and the safety of employees from any element of the political or societal environment. Czinkota, Ronkainen, and Moffett incorporate in political risk both "the actions of legitimate government authorities" and "events caused by factors outside the control of government."[5] The latter clearly moves sources of political risk into the social realm.

On a practical level, it is necessary to employ a more comprehensive definition of what constitutes political risk and political loss. Specifically, any functional definition of political risk has to include acts and attributes that reflect societal sources—including international society—as well as national governmental origins. Negative government actions that are not insurable should be covered. Actions against businesses that derive from the society that are insurable under political risk

---

[2] Janice Monti-Belkaoui and Ahmed Riahi-Belkaoui, *The Nature, Estimation, and Management of Political Risk*, Westport, CN: Quorum Books, 1998, pp. 15-112.

[3] Betty Jane Punnett and David A. Ricks, *International Business*, Belmont, CA: Wadsworth Publishing Co., 1992, p. 187.

[4] Ricky W. Griffin and Michael W. Pustay, *International Business: A Managerial Perspective, 2nd Edition*, Reading, MA: Addison-Wesley, 1998, pp. 309-310.

[5] Michael R. Czinkota, Ilkka A. Ronkainen, and Michael Moffett, *International Business—Update 2000*, Fort Worth: The Dryden Press, 2000, p. 107.

insurance must be covered. And by extension, many acts generated within a society against a foreign investor, although perhaps not covered by insurance, should also be counted in the political category. These include general strikes intended to bring down a government that stop production at an assembly plant, rioting between two ethnic groups that results in deaths of trained employees, or a kidnapping of a manager by guerrillas raising money for their political war.

To summarize, losses that can be described as resulting from political causes can be the result of government decisions or societal conditions, of national government or lower level government decisions, of characteristics of the country or characteristics of the investing firm, or combinations of all of these. Any model that examines only one of these types is probably not useful for a specific firm.

Let's approach this question another way. Losses are the outcome of high and uncontrolled political risk. Losses that can affect either the physical investment or cross-border financing and that evolve from political or societal sources include a range of particular types.[6] These types can be broken down into eight categories.

> *Inconvertibility* – an action taken by a government to prevent conversion of local currency to some form of foreign exchange such as dollars. This is also referred to as "transfer risk."

> *Expropriation or Nationalization* – where a government seizes property or assets of the foreign investor without full compensation to the investor. It is also called "ownership risk."

> *Civil Strife Damage* – property or income losses from domestic political violence. Includes hostile actions by national forces, civil war, revolution, insurrection, or politically motivated terrorism or sabotage.

> *War Damage* – property or income losses resulting from an international conflict. May include declared or undeclared war. Both civil strife damage and war damage can be considered as categories of ownership risk.

---

[6] Llewellyn D. Howell, "Country and Political Risk Analysis: Foundations for Foreign Direct Investment," in L. D. Howell, ed., *The Handbook of Country and Political Risk Analysis*, 2nd Edition, East Syracuse, NY: The PRS Group, 1998, pp. 3-4.

Contract Repudiation – sometimes called "breach of contract" this loss results from government termination of contracts without compensation for existing investment in the product or service.

Negative Government Actions – where a government might formally decide to reduce or restrict earnings or the participation of foreign investors in ways that are less direct than expropriation or inconvertibility. An example would be when a government decides to place a tax on foreigners resident in the jurisdiction but not on citizens of the host country. These can also be considered a form of "operations risk."

Losses from Process Deterioration – losses resulting from indirect government action. Such factors as government attributes (rather than decisions) and societal processes or characteristics. (e.g., lack of enforcement of copyright agreements, an inefficient judicial system that can't process claims, bribery and systemic corruption that the government cannot or will not control, high general crime rates uncontrolled by the government).

Losses from Event Intervention – a loss that results from some event that is political in its nature or source, while not being a result of known government decision (i.e., the kidnapping of managers or executives, strikes or production stoppages that have political rather than economic or financial objectives, sabotage or damage to a plant or service that originates with a political or religious group in the host country).

These eight categories include all of the types listed with the insurance coverage definition but also include other instances that can reasonably be said to be political. If these all can be identified as losses that we count in the "political" category, and if they cover the complete range of losses of this type, political risk will be those causal decisions, factors, or conditions that often lead to such losses.

Political Risk Forecasting: Multiple Approaches

Risk refers to the presence of a condition that could cause or facilitate a loss to a foreign investor such as those cited above. The key question is then what are the conditions that lead to these losses. Risk models, like the *Economist*, BERI, and ICRG models, are composed of the political and social characteristics of a host country that the model builders thought result—singly or in combination—in one or more of the eight loss types. The nature of the variables, the number of variables included, and the weights assigned to the variables (a model) are a result of the theory held by the model builders. That is, the causal model is the result of political risk *analysis*.

Unfortunately, we often find that the terms assessment and analysis are used interchangeably for both country and political risk, although they actually have different (although related) objectives. Political risk *assessment* is a measure, in this case a probability measure, that acts as a warning of *level* of threat. In political risk *analysis*, the origins or causes of the threat—whatever its level—are the object of attention. This attempt to delineate causality is the theoretical aspect of political risk that is often neglected.[7] In fact, theory is often absent or at least not explicit for models used in forecasting political risk. Variables seem sometimes to be chosen because they are hot issues or come readily to mind among the originators of a model.

We need to recognize that *every process of analysis and assessments that are derived from them are dependent on underlying theory about the causes of politically sourced losses*. The theory determines what kind of predictive variables are examined, how they are measured, and how they are combined to generate an overall risk rating. Although theories are seldom explicated by the various ratings systems, they exist nevertheless and can usually be derived from an examination of the system or model utilized.

Although we lack systematic studies of most of the existing models, it is possible to get at information about what is useful to managers by surveying the models that are and have been in use by professional risk assessment firms and by industries and firms heavily involved in the global economy. We undertake this examination with this logic in mind: by starting with the loss categories and working backward, knowing the source variables that are in regular use and for which there is data, and making the connection between sources and particular types of losses, a firm's management can determine which causal variables they should be alert to by knowing which types of losses can affect their specific firm. As will be noted again below, most political risk assessments are made for countries as a whole and for

---

[7] Several such efforts to explore models for their utility can be found in Llewellyn D. Howell and Brad Chaddick, "Models of Political Risk for Foreign Investment and Trade: An Assessment of Three Approaches," *Columbia Journal of World Business*, Vol. XXIX, No. 3, Fall 1994, pp. 70-91 and in Llewellyn D. Howell, "Governmental Attributes in Political Risk," in this volume.

foreign investors in general. Whether they apply to a specific firm, on a specific project, in a specific part of the country is questionable. But the data can be adapted for much narrower use. This latter effort is my intention here.

Listed in Table A (below) are 14 unique political risk assessments produced by 12 different firms. The variables employed in producing political risk assessments have been divided into two tables, utilizing the system "code" in Table A. Figure 1 lists those with attribute configurations included in the model. Figure 2 lists those with government decision factors.

The 14 ratings systems, between them, list 33 attribute variables and 11 decision variables. Table B (next page) lists those variables.

The only model that is explicitly directed at government decision-making is the

Table A: 14 Key Political Risk Assessments	Codes (in Fig 1 & 2)
The PRS Group, Inc.	
International Country Risk Guide	ICRG
Political Risk Services	PRS
Business Environment Risk Intelligence (BERI) S.A.	
Political Risk Index	BPRI
Operational Risk Index	BORI
Economist Intelligence Unit	EIU
Moody's Investor Services	MIS
Control Risks Group	CRG
Economists' Method – 1986	E-86
S.J. Rundt & Associates	SJR
Standard & Poor's Ratings Group	S&P
Institutional Investor	II
Chase – 1988	C-88
IHS Energy Group	IHS
Euromoney	Euro

model employed by Political Risk Services (the Coplin-O'Leary model) of The PRS Group. The *Euromoney* model focuses exclusively on the risk of non-payment of

Table B: **Political Risk Attributes** **& Decision Variables**	Codes (Fig. 1)
General "Political Risk"	A
External Factors	
Influence of Major Powers	B
Negative Regional Influences	C
International War	D
International Economic Alliances	E
Nature of Government & Politics	
Nature of Politics	F
Stability	G
Authoritarianism	H
Legitimacy	I
Political Parties	J
Political Opposition Forces	K
Staleness	L
Military Involved in Politics	M
Religion in Politics	N
Corruption	O
Regulatory Investment Environment	P
Judicial/Legal System	Q
Government Behavior	R
Political Intrusion on Wealth Cultivation	S
Political Intrusion on Economic Management	T
Societal Character	
Ethnic Tension	U
Socioeconomic Conditions	V
Domestic Violence Civil Conflict	W
Bureaucracy Quality	X
Nationalism	Y
Attitudes Toward Foreigners	Z
Environmental Activism	AA
Domestic Economic Problems	BB
International Economic Problems	CC
Infrastructure	DD
Professional Services & Contractors	EE
Local Management & Partners	FF
Culture	GG

debt for loans, goods, and services. The other 12 models are heavily slanted toward the use of attributes in forecasting threats to investors. These attributes fall into three clear-cut categories: 1) external factors; 2) the nature of government and politics; and 3) societal character. Among these attributes, the nature of government and politics gets the most attention, but societal character follows closely. This is consistent with the broad definition suggested above. It is important to note, however, that external factors are given serious attention, appearing in nine of the 14 models examined. If external variables were combined with societal, this unified category would dominate. As a matter of historical application, this would tell us that the environmental variables were more important in practice that those directly related to government and politics. But both are obviously needed. It may well be, too, that the variables related to the environment have an influence on government decisions that in turn is directed at the foreign investor. These linkages need to be investigated.

In Figures 1 and 2, on the following pages, first the attributes (separated into the three groups) and then the decisions are presented in the order of their usage in these models. Only those with more frequent inclusion are listed. In Figure 3, a speculative match-up is made between the loss categories and the likely causal variables that relate to it. Our objective, in a moment, will be to match a firm's particular vulnerabilities with an assessed situation. First, let's look again at the purpose of these identifications.

Forecasts such as political risk assessments are intended to provide some basis for determining the need for political risk insurance or other means of managing or mitigating the risk of losses that are due to particular political characteristics or actions in the host country. Insurance coverage by agencies such as OPIC or MIGA set attributes of loss types that meet the criterion of "political." These include losses due to inconvertibility, expropriation or nationalization, war damage, civil strife damage, and contract repudiation by governments (see the list above). Lloyd's, AIG, and other private insurance firms cover these and other political risks with contracts specific to the risk faced. But the specific risk being faced must be known since the contracts must be specific to the potential loss.

With regard to the host country, there are three theoretical divisions that need to be considered. The first is that theories are divided into those that attribute causality to (A) an underlying *attribute configuration* and conditions in the country, versus those that take (B) a more "rational actor" or *government decision-making* approach. BERI, ICRG, and EIU, for example, rely on underlying conditions such as the level of Ethnic fractionalization or the extent of democracy present in the host country government.

PRS, on the other hand, focuses explicitly on national government decisions such as those relating to levels of nontariff barriers, repatriation restrictions, or operations interference. The Euromoney assessment is based on the perceived likelihood that governments will repay debt, a rather singular reliance on government decision-making.

There is no reason that the two should not be combined, and they are in some cases. Political risk in a country could be the combination of both a government's inclination to interfere in operations *and* the presence of ethnic division and strife. A more important theoretical question is whether special national circumstances—such as a dominant religious culture that emphasizes a hierarchical ruling system (e.g., "Islamic Fundamentalism" in the *Economist* model)—coincide with a decision type (e.g., "Operations Restrictions" from the PRS model. It could be argued that characteristics are a causal factor in particular decisions.

Similarly, in political risk analysis we have to be concerned about relationships among the variables in the assessment model. Several models, for example (ICRG, *The Economist*), include both extent of democracy and involvement of the military in politics as separate variables in calculating the assessment. It can be easily argued that these two variables are so interrelated that they are really one. Including them both in an assessment would therefore be tantamount to counting the same variable twice, therefore distorting the assessment. These questions must be addressed in the theory phase of building risk assessment systems but usually are not.

The second theoretical division is that between approaches described as either (C) *macro* or (D) *micro*. This division has been characterized in several ways but usually with reference to macro analysis as being concerned with government decisions that would relate to all foreign investors in a country, while micro analysis is addressing "government policies and actions that influence selected sectors of the economy or specific foreign businesses in the country."[8] The latter would include assessments related to particular firms. While the macro/micro differentiation is usually discussed in the context of government decisions, it can be applied as well to country characteristics, where, for example, ethnic divisions in a country might affect manufacturing facilities but wouldn't have any direct effect on financial investors in host country stock markets.

A third division that must be considered is the unit level for either characteristics or government decisions. We might divide this into categories (E) *national* and (F) *local*, although this is really a spectrum that could be divided much more finely. As we know well in the case of the United States, there may be cases where the national government does not interfere in foreign investment but a state or local government does. In Vietnam, there are government divisions that run from national to provincial to city or even village, with a variety of policies. The differentiation applies to risk characteristics as well, where, for example, corruption may be denounced and inhibited at the national level while it is rampant at some local levels (but not necessarily others).

---

[8]Richard M. Hodgetts and Fred Luthans, *International Management*, New York: McGraw-Hill, Inc., 1991, pp. 118-119.

Figure 1: Risk in Attribute Configuration

	ICRG	PRS	BPRI	BORI	EIU	MIS	CRG	E-86	SJ	S&P	II	C-88	IHS
A											▓		
External Factors													
B			▓					▓		▓		▓	
C			▓		▓		▓	▓		▓			
D	▓				▓					▓			▓
E						▓							
Nature of Government & Politics													
F									▓	▓			
G	▓		▓	▓			▓	▓		▓		▓	▓
H	▓		▓		▓		▓	▓					
I						▓	▓						
J			▓										
K			▓										
L								▓					
M	▓						▓	▓					
N													
O	▓		▓		▓		▓	▓				▓	
P	▓												
Q				▓		▓							
R						▓							
S									▓				
T		▓		▓		▓			▓				
Societal Character													
U	▓		▓				▓	▓					▓
V	▓	▓	▓				▓		▓			▓	
W	▓	▓	▓		▓				▓				▓
X				▓	▓								
Y			▓										
Z			▓	▓	▓				▓				
AA													▓
BB		▓					▓						
CC		▓											
DD				▓		▓							
EE				▓									
FF				▓									
GG			▓	▓	▓								

Figure 2: Risk in Government Decisions

	PRS	BORI	SJR	IHS	Euro
General "Political Risk"					Risk of non-payment of debt for loans, goods, services
Equity Restrictions	Restrictions on equity holdings		Risk of ex-propriation w/o full com-pensation	Constraints on foreign oil company in-vestment	
Taxation System and Problems	Taxation dis-crimination				
Repatriation Restric-tions	Repatriation Restrictions			Restrictions on repatria-tion/ converti-bility	
Exchange Controls	Exchange Controls				
Changes in Con-tracts/Fiscal Terms				Threat of adverse changes in contracts/ fiscal terms	
Added Tariff Barriers	Tariff Barriers				
Added Nontariff Bar-riers	Nontariff Bar-riers				
Payment Delays	Payment De-lays				
Labor Costs	Labor costs	Labor cost/ productivity	Labor-management relations		
Foreign Debt	Foreign debt				

Political Risk Assessment: Operationalization and Application

The "foreign investor" that is the recipient of the risk information implies at least two entities. The first is the obvious, the firm with a project to be undertaken in a foreign environment. The second is the financial institution(s) that provides the capital that underpins the direct investment. The source of risk to both is the same, with the effect passed through the investor to the lender. Both should be looking for risk sources in their examination of a potential investment environment. What do they look for? Let's use the IHS Energy Group example.

Companies in the petroleum exploration and production field are almost always going to be located in less developed sections of a country or offshore. If they expect to be working on land and away from urban centers, they will be (and have been) particularly vulnerable to civil strife damage. Such companies in South America and Africa have, in recent years, had employees attacked, expat managers kidnapped, pipelines tapped by thieves or blown up by guerrillas, and facilities destroyed in battles between government and rebel forces. How can they anticipate this kind of damage?

In Figure 3 there are three examples of how attributes and decisions from risk models can be matched up with the loss categories, five of which are directly insurable. The second example is directly related to the interests of a company like IHS that serves a petroleum industry. IHS recognized that a major vulnerability existed in its need to operate in remote locations, away from the protection afforded by larger cities and proximity to the seat of government and the military protection that it might entail. It saw that the primary political risk that its clients might face would be civil strife damage.

Beginning with that assumption, IHS constructed a model with three components: a Political Risks Index, a Socio-Economic Risks Index, and a Commercial Petroleum Risks Index. What IHS saw as "political risk" was clearly the political violence that might arise in areas where the petroleum industry would be working.

Their Political Risks Index is composed of four attributes, all common among the models examined above. They include 1) war and external threats—including issues of sovereignty and border disputes, 2) civil and labor unrest—including

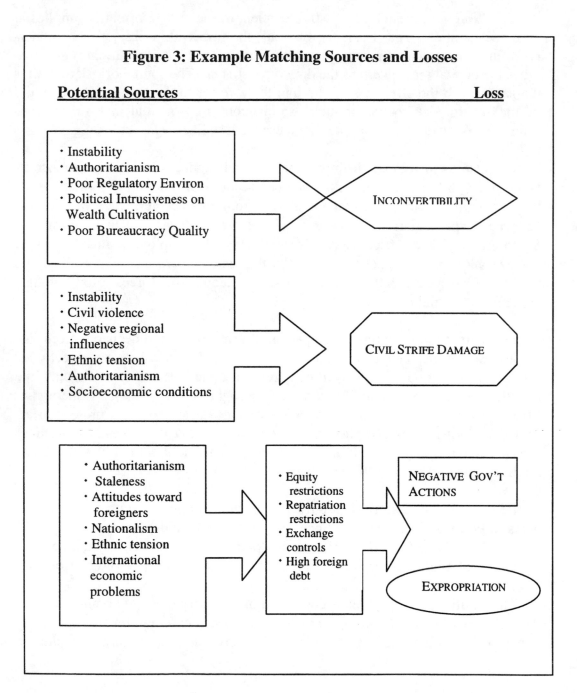

Figure 3: Example Matching Sources and Losses

Potential Sources   **Loss**

- Instability
- Authoritarianism
- Poor Regulatory Environ
- Political Intrusiveness on Wealth Cultivation
- Poor Bureaucracy Quality

INCONVERTIBILITY

- Instability
- Civil violence
- Negative regional influences
- Ethnic tension
- Authoritarianism
- Socioeconomic conditions

CIVIL STRIFE DAMAGE

- Authoritarianism
- Staleness
- Attitudes toward foreigners
- Nationalism
- Ethnic tension
- International economic problems

- Equity restrictions
- Repatriation restrictions
- Exchange controls
- High foreign debt

NEGATIVE GOV'T ACTIONS

EXPROPRIATION

strikes, protests, and demonstrations against the government, 3) internal violence as evidenced by bombings, assassinations, kidnappings, low-intensity guerrilla warfare, and crime, and 4) regime instability as indicated in either regularly scheduled changes or unanticipated events such as a coup or death.[9] In addition, the Socio-Economic Risks Index contains a variable "Ethno-Linguistic Factionalism" that is common to many other models in the form of "Ethnic Tension" (ICRG) or "Ethnic Fractionalization" (BERI ORI). It is also interesting to note that the IHS method also includes a breakdown into regions within the country, where some regions are more dangerous for petroleum investors than others. This structure could easily accommodate a differentiation between the risks found in national and local governments.

The five indicators seem logically and certainly anecdotally related to subsequent civil strife, in areas of a country where oil producers would be operating. IHS has selectively employed common indicators among those for which data is readily available and has enabled an assessment that serves the immediate interests of particular firms. At minimum, where such risks are high, the petroleum firms must seek out and obtain Civil Strife Damage insurance. For American firms, this is readily available from OPIC and MIGA.

Any investing firm can employ a similar approach. A financial investor without in-country facilities would be little interested in attributes that portend civil strife, but would be more concerned about the nature and quality of the government, its leadership, and stability in the international economic system. Looking at inconvertibility and its origins would be a more appropriate direction of interest.

A Concluding Note

There are several informational goals in this article, which can be presented in a few summary points. First, political risk assessment is a practice that is widely in use today, necessarily so in a global environment that is full of dangers for an increasingly large number of international investors. Second, there is a diversity of approaches to assessing political risk, mainly divided between governmental and societal theories of the origins of risk. However, there is no need to exclusively pick one or the other. Third, data on these important investment environ-

---

[9] Terry Hallmark and Kevin Whited, "The IHS Energy Group's 'Political Risk Ratings and Ranking Index," in Llewellyn D. Howell, ed., *The Handbook of Country and Political Risk Analysis, 3rd Edition*, East Syracuse, NY: The PRS Group, 2001, Chap. 12.

ment attributes are available from a number of commercial and private firms that regularly produce them. And fourth, although the data are usually created for use in country-level assessments, individual investors can select among the variables and reconstruct models that fit the particular needs of that firm. Every firm can identify which country attributes and decisions should be of concern to them by backtracking from their major vulnerabilities to the causal sources of linked losses.

Politically based losses do not appear out of the blue. The signs are always there. All we have to do is know where to look for them and what to do with them once we've found them. Political risk assessment can work for you in improving investment success and profitability.

Chapter 2

Approaches to Political Risk Analysis
Walter Molano

Introduction

The modern international system is a collection of states and transnational actors, such as multinational corporations and individual investors. This system is based on a principle of sovereignty or self-rule, meaning that each state develops its own independent policies. Politics is immediately associated with power and authority; however, its meaning may be extended to the macro dimension of nation-states of territoriality, sovereignty and jurisdiction (Arbeláez, 1993). Although there is global cooperation on many issues, there is no world government or police force. Fluctuating national policies can complicate long term economic projects, such as loans or direct investments. Although military or diplomatic action may compel a foreign country to respect the existing property rights of investors, the social costs of using such force may make this action prohibitive. Therefore, the risk of political action is an important factor which must be added to the other economic risk factors when considering investments in the international arena. This paper examines the concept of political risk and the leading methods of evaluating it.

Although political risk assessment has grown into a multi-million dollar industry. Providers of political risk services have been faced with the complex task of conveying large quantities of information. Some of them chose to use esoteric and elegant quantitative techniques to simplify the presentation of political factors. The proliferation of quantitative measurement models have under-emphasized the complexity of political analysis.

Political Risk Analysis

The role of political information in international commercial activity is as ancient as international commerce. The Greek City-States established a consulate system in neighboring countries to file regular reports on the political events which were affecting trade activity. Economic intelligence was always a part of the diplomatic corps, but the rapid increase in the flow of private investment took the role of economic information gathering out of the hands of the state and put into the hands of individual companies. The modern format of systematic appraisal of government stability was developed by Root (1968). He argued that information on political stability was a critical factor in shaping attitudes toward investment.

Increased global interdependence in the 1970s expanded opportunities for multinationals, banks and investors. From 1965 to 1980 exports from high income countries grew at an annual rate of 7.3% (World Bank, 1992). But interdependence also increased exposure to foreign political risk. Researchers and investors became interested in the elements of risk which were inherent in the economic, social and political environment of doing business in other countries (Kennedy, 1987). In order to understand and evaluate political risk it is best to discuss its meaning, characteristics, and dimensions.

What is political risk? Political risk can be defined as the broad spectrum of actions in the political and social environment which can influence a transnational actor's property rights, income or market. A review of the literature on political risk since the 1960s suggested several definitions. Root (1968) proposed that political risk was represented by threats to foreign investments that could arise from the attitudes and behavior of governments and social groups. Robock (1970) operationalized political risk in the following terms:

...Political risk in international business exists (1) when discontinuities occur in the business environment, (2) when they are difficult to anticipate and (3) when they result from political change. To constitute a "risk" these changes in the business environment must have a potential for significantly affecting the profit or other goals of a particular enterprise.

Haendel, West and Meadow (1975) defined political risk as

...the risk or probability of occurrence of some political event(s) that will change the prospects for the profitability of a given investment.

In the extreme form, political risk is the confiscation of property known as nationalization or expropriation.1 This type of action has obliterated billions of dollars in multinational assets, and the relatively recent cases of Iran and Chile left

---

[1] Countries rarely resort to such extreme actions since it impedes future chances to participate in the world economy.

an indelible mark on the boards of all multinationals. But the incidence of expropriation is relatively low. There are many other political actions which can affect the performance of a project. For example, the decision to change the taxation rate of income earned by foreign investors is a form of political risk; likewise, the political decision to limit the repatriation of money by multinationals is another form of political risk.2 Another situation which creates risk is political drift. Governments experiencing drift are too weak, preoccupied or corrupt to enact necessary policies. The result can be instability or anarchic conditions. These non-market forces ultimately affect corporate cash flow and the value of a foreign investment. Therefore, political risk refers to situations where foreign governments can alter either legal title to property or the value of an investment.3

It is important to note that although there were distinctions between political risk and country risk. The former focusing on political events, such as social activism, nationalizations, and popular revolutions, while the latter focusing on longer term national characteristics, such as demographics and historical antecedents. The devastating impact of the Third World debt crisis on various levels and types of international commercial activity obscured the distinction between the two risks and made them synonymous concepts (Arbeláez, 1993).

In order to understand political risk, it is necessary to categorize the ways political events can affect project performance. One suggestion is to divide political events along two dimensions (Kennedy, 1991).4 The first dimension is a continuum between legal and extralegal events. Legal incidents are those which comply with established laws.5 Although events may be categorized as being

---

[2]Other forms of political risk include the frenzy of nationalizations and exchange control regulations in France after the socialist government took control in 1981; the refusal of the Brazilian government to enforce copy-right and product infringement laws in computer technology; price freezes and controls in Argentina; arbitrary refusals to access to certain geographic market in Japan (Freidmann and Kim, 1988).

[3]It is important to note that political risk does not just have a negative connotation. It is also an opportunity for an investor to capture high returns and the greatest rewards go to investors which can best assess and manage the risk.

[4]Arbeláez (1993) proposed another way to categorize political risk by framing the theories of political risk within six general approaches: the actor/source approach, the relative deprivation approach, the product/venture-type approach, and the government approach. This classification schema is presented in Table I.

[5]A drawback of this categorization is that governments constantly redefine what is legal.

legal, they may result in political risk. An example of a legal event is a democratic election which may give rise to a political party which is hostile to foreign firms. Extralegal events are actions which occur outside the legal structure. Examples of extralegal events are kidnapping, sabotage, or military coups. The second dimension of political events is the level of incident. A macro level event is an action which impacts all foreign business activity. Likewise, a micro level event is an action which impacts individual activities.

The combination of the two dimensions allows analysts to categorize and evaluate political events as they may impact business activity (See Figure 1). This format allows firms to evaluate their risk exposure and dedicate resources to improve information gathering in those areas.

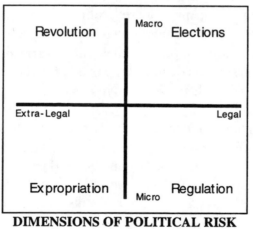

DIMENSIONS OF POLITICAL RISK
(FIGURE 1)

Another suggested categorization of political risk creates a division between events and actors (Ascher, 1982). Elections, wars, or policy choices are discrete events which can have an important impact on the status of investments, but just as important are the small additive events which transform the structure of society. Likewise, national level actors can make pivotal choices, but grass-root movements by atomistic actors can create powerful social changes. This approach categorizes political risk along a dimension which focuses on scope and provides a framework for investors to assess their political risk coverage.

Methods of Evaluating Political Risk

The expansion of global economic activity in the post-war period was paralleled by the steady growth of theoretically-based political risk analysis. The unforeseen events of the late 1960s and 70s further highlighted the link between politics and economics (Simon, 1982). Events which struck a blow to multinationals, such as the Arab Oil Boycott and the Iranian Revolution, led to an explosion in risk services and experts--many of which were not theoretically-based. A new multi-million dollar cottage industry of 'experts' emerged from academic institutions to hawk political risk models. In order to examine and evaluate the many methods of assessing political risk it is necessary to establish three criteria--level of comparability, ability to predict and timeliness.

Comparability: Given that multinationals and investors desire to maximize the rewards of investing, they seek information which allows the comparison of returns in different countries. These formats have been used in the computation of financial evaluations. Numeric formats allow political risks to be incorporated into decision-making models, such as capital budgeting, which calculate payback period, discount rate or projected cash flows.6 Numeric data can also be manipulated into models to evaluate trends, but numeric formats are simpler in concept than in practice. Social and political variables require operationalization, measurement and quantification. Many of the factors involved in political risk analysis, such as political stability or hostility to foreigners are not amenable to measurement or quantification. The absence of absolute scales in these topics leads to the use of arbitrary quantifications.7 Failure to employ rigorous standards in operationalization of social and political variables can result in dangerously faulty analysis, over-simplification or comparisons which are false. Quantitative methods not only eliminate contextual analysis, they build exogenous factors into the structure of their models. The problem is that when the exogenous factors change, then the model fails to operate.

Predictability: Past patterns of behavior are important considerations in political risk analysis, but investors are especially keen on knowing how future events will affect their projects. The growth of statistical modeling has allowed many political risk analysts to make forecasting claims. Econometric models take past

---

[6] It is important to note that numeric formats require a theory which connects the numbers to the parameters of the financial evaluation. The fundamental objection to quantitative risk indicators is that they do not correspond to any meaningful elements of financial or other decision-making evaluations (Ascher, 1978).

[7] In addition to problems with measurement, there are significant problems with data collection. Compatible cross-national data is often not available and countries have been known to lie about macro-economic indicators. Data problems also occur due to problems with definition. For example, unemployment definitions vary greatly across countries.

patterns or trends and make linear or non-linear predictions. Methods like regression and extrapolation can give viable predictions when the political and economic system is stable; yet when there is instability in the system, the forecasting model must correspond to some sort of theoretical concept. Under these conditions statistical correlations are useless unless they explain the relationship between two events. In other words, predictions are best when they are bolstered by theories which explain why certain events produce other events.

Timeliness: The third characteristic of political risk analysis is timeliness. Major international events unfold slowly, develop subtly and change course with maddening unpredictability. But the value of information decays rapidly with time, political risk analysis must use the latest available information and provide information to users in a timely fashion. Political analysis must be in a format which provides for continuous coverage but allows users to incorporate risk analysis into timely decisions.

Four General Approaches to Political Risk: A *Harvard Business Review* survey of political risk suggested four general categories of analysis--Old Hands, Delphi, Quantitative and Grand Tour (Rummel and Heenan, 1978). We will place the major forms of analysis into these general categories and analyze them according to the above criteria of comparability, predictability and timeliness.[8] Finally, we will plot the different forms of analysis along the two dimensional format suggested by Kennedy (1991).

Old Hands: The first category is called old hands because it employs expert opinions from professionals with a high level of experience in a particular country. Most of these services are provided by individuals from academia, media or government on an ad-hoc basis, but some individuals like Kissinger Associates have created consulting firms with regular newsletters to support clients. The comparability of these services tend to be low because experts usually focus on only one country or region. Yet, the predictability of this method tends to be high. Country experts usually employ implicit models which interpret data and trends into reliable forecasts. Experts use judgement and experience to process large quantities and qualities of data. The timeliness of the old hands method also tends to be good--if a permanent relationship has been established. Country experts tend to have real-time connections with the countries they cover. Due to the

---

[8]It is important to note that the political risk assessment industry is volatile. There is a high level of turnover in firms and personnel.

complexity of the international environment and the importance of international markets, the use of consultants has been growing (Rogers, 1992). Rogers found that the paring away of corporate staffs created a need for external consultants specialized in niche areas which were beyond the capabilities of the firm. A survey of 18 multinational firms conducted by Stapenhurst (1993) found that the use of external consultants was growing (see Table II).

Delphi: The second approach is the Delphi technique. This approach builds on the old hands method by polling various experts through a common format. It is a technique for organizing expert opinion. Experts provide ratings to different political risks and then qualify their answers. The two major firms using this approach are Business International and Business Environmental Risk Index. Business International (BI) (also known as the Country Assessment Service) has been in operation since 1971 and uses hundreds of experts in over 70 countries. The BI stability index rates each country from 2 to 15. The range represents different risk potentials from long-term stability to strong possibility of overthrow. Business Environmental Risk Index (BERI) has been in operation since 1966 and reviews 45 countries. Over a hundred volunteer panelists from industry, banks, and government rate fifteen factors that affect the business climate on a scale from 0 to 4. The factors are then weighted so that the highest possible sum is 100. Each panelist rates five to ten countries for a period of six to twelve months in the future. Although Delphi methods use numeric formats, their operationalization of variables is questionable. There is often a lack of consensus between the panelists in the terms of definitions and classification of political risk. Absence of an explicit model also obscures the predictability of method. Delphi models are also not very timely. They usually are published on a quarterly basis, which is far from a real time appraisal of political risks.

Quantitative: Quantitative approaches employ macro-level statistics to generate models of political risk. Quantitative methods vary in degree of complexity from relatively simplistic checklists to complex econometric models. One of the first models is the Political Risk Index (PRI) which was introduced in 1973 by Douglas Hibbs. The PRI model uses factor and regression analysis to measure political instability. Many variables, such as riots, strikes, and violent deaths, are used to measure the probability of collective protest or internal war. PRI employs a numeric format which is amenable to comparisons and implementation in financial models. It also uses variables which are derived from qualitative theories about political change and stability, but it is as timely as the BI and BERI formats.

The Rummel and Heenan's categories are not exhaustive and there are other forms of evaluating political risk. A second group of quantitative services are those which cater to financial clients. ***Euromoney*** and ***Institutional Investor*** provide information on the credit-worthiness of countries (Jalilvand, 1987).[9] Since 1979, ***Euromoney*** has published an annual Country Risk League Table which ranks sovereign borrowers active in the Eurocurrency market (see Appendix A). Borrowers are classified on the basis of the average weighted spread the country was able to obtain in a given year (Heffernan, 1986).[10] The ***Institutional Investor*** rankings (see Appendix B) are based on a survey technique where 75 to 100 banks are asked to grade the credit-worthiness of a country on a scale of 0 (greatest probability of default) to 100 (lowest probability of default).[11] Although these rankings employ a numeric format, they only compare countries that are active in the loan market.[12] Although these services are designed to maximize comparability in credit risk, they do not give any forecasting. Furthermore, this service is the least timely, since the tables are usually published once or twice a year.[13]

---

[9] The bond rating agencies also provide risk ratings for individual countries. Ratings for stock or bond issues in a particular country can never exceed the rating for the country--regardless of their credit.

[10] The formula for the determination of a country's average weighted spread is

$$\frac{\Sigma(\text{volume} * \text{spread} * \text{maturity})}{\Sigma(\text{volume} * \text{maturity})}$$

The volume measures all loans in a given year on the Eurodollar and DM syndicated markets. The spread is the margin over LIBOR and maturity is the prime over which the loan matures. Those countries with lowest spreads are ranked highest in the league table, since the lower the spread the lower the risk.

11 The responses are weighted according to the size of the bank's sovereign loan exposure and the sophistication of its sovereign loan risk techniques. Readers are not provided with the weighted formula.

[12] Country risk ratings are not a unified construct. They reduce the entire country into a single risk category. Yet, there are often very safe and unrisky individual projects in countries with poor risk ratings.

[13] A variation of this approach is the currency substitution method. This approach gages political risk by measuring the use of foreign currency (Agmon, 1985). Although the premise of this methodology assumes that people in countries with high political risk will not hold the currency, it does not account for situations where there is alot of international trade or foreign currency is being used to stabilize the home currency, such as the dollarization of the Argentine peso.

A hybrid approach which has gained significant media attention is Political Risk Services (PRS). This is a newsletter which combines the Delphi and quantitative approach. This service provides 85 country reports that produce forecasts based on country expert opinions and macro-economic data. The reports provide both numeric and qualitative analysis. It also furnishes a 6, 12 and 18 month forecast on regime stability, government policy and economic performance. Although monthly reports are not real-time, they do provide an up-to-date assessment.

Grand Tour: A major deficiency of the three former categories of political risk analysis is their macro focus. These methods are built on the problematic assumption that each firm in a country faces the same level of political risk. In reality, projects differ in their susceptibilities to political risk, depending on their size, composition of ownership, level of technology, and other factors.[14] One way to enrich the micro focus is through the grand tour. The first hand experience of visiting a country and assessing the political climate allows investors to examine the specific micro-level factors which may impact their project. Nonetheless, the grand tour relies heavily on subjective interpretation. This type of experience has been criticized by proponents of quantitative methods because subjective methods complicate comparability, since cultural differences often cloud perceptions.[15] It is also a poor format to conducting forecasts.

Numerous banks and multinationals built on the concept of in-house expertise by incorporating political risk assessment teams into the corporate structure. The investment bank, Salomon Brothers, has an extensive research staff led by a political scientist who monitors the politics and economics of countries. They use a four step strategy which focuses on national policies, macro-economic indicators, balance-of-payments, and liquid reserves.[16] Multinationals have also

---

[14] For example or creeping expropriation is more likely to occur in the extractive, utility, and financial services of an economy rather than the manufacturing sector (Vernon, 1977).

[15] Proponents of subjective methods have countered that all quantitative models incorporate subjective elements. Models are designed with assumptions and characteristics which produce answers which are in-line with the modeler's expectations. Therefore, why tamper with expert judgement at all (Ascher, 1989)?

[16] The in-house research staff at Salomon concluded that sovereign default of on debt is usually linked to an inability to pay and not a political unwillingness. Cases of willingness to pay generally take place in an environment of extreme political instability or open hostilities and when the political

developed independent teams and models. Two popular political risk models are Shell Oil's ASPRO SPAIR and American Can's PRISM. Oil company teams have also pioneered the use of scenarios to model the effects of political-economic events on oil prices. The value of in-house teams is enhanced by their ability to provide a broad spectrum of information to high-level decision makers. While in-house groups can provide real-time analysis and forecasting dedicated to specific macro and micro areas of interest, they are very costly to implement.

Mapping of Political Risk Analysis

The two dimensional conceptualization of political risk analysis suggested by Kennedy (1991) provides an interesting format to view the different type of services (See Figure 2).

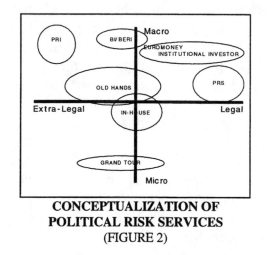

CONCEPTUALIZATION OF POLITICAL RISK SERVICES
(FIGURE 2)

As stated above, in-house political services can provide the best services, but their prohibitive cost may force the mixed use of other types of risk assessment services. Decision makers employing political risk analysis must first understand their own needs and match them to the appropriate services. This will allow them to design an efficient, yet effective, approach.

Managing Political risk

It is important to note that in addition to obtaining passive information on political risks, multinationals and investors can also take several pro-active

---

leadership rejects the integration of their country in to the system of global capital flows (Purcell, 1993).

actions to manage political risks. The first is to obtain more and better information. Decision-makers should be provided with constant updates on changes and developments in countries. Diversity of information sources should be a major consideration when gathering data. Often foreign branches of the company give a tainted view of the situation in order to suit personal career goals.

The second method to manage political risk is to incorporate risk into the financial equation. This would set investment thresholds which would account for the various risks. The third method is to apply portfolio theory to international investments. In addition to a weighting of risk Betas, this method suggests the diversification of projects along sectors and location. Many firms have scattered production across several countries to prevent the capture of an industry through nationalization. The fourth method suggests the use of insurance programs. The Overseas Private Investment Corporation (OPIC) provides coverage for U.S. investments in friendly lesser-developed countries. The Multilateral Investment Guarantee Agency (MIGA) is a member of the World Bank Group and it also insures investment activity in developing countries. The last method is to take preemptive steps to decrease political risk.[17]

Conclusion

Political risk analysis is an important tool for multinationals and individual investors conducting business abroad, but users of this information must understand the limitation of the services. It is a method reducing vast quantities of data into a useful format. Users of political risk assessment services should be skeptical of quantitative methods. They should view the approaches as a tool, but not a philosophers stone.

Decision makers should obtain services which maximize their information and they should avail themselves to the maximum amount of diversified information. They should also take steps to manage their risk and lever the highest return from their information. Political risk analysis should not only be used as a method of avoiding problems, but as a method of discovering and properly pricing rewarding opportunities.

---

[17] Firms must also understand that actions in their home country may result in political reactions which will place projects at risk (Sethi and Luther, 1986).

Table I:
Classification Schema for Political Risk Analysis
(Friedmann and Kim, 1988 and Arbeláez, 1993)

Approach	Tenet	Proponent (Year)
1. *Frustration-Aggression and Relative Deprivation*	National frustration; discrepancy between value expectation and value capabilities; violence societal behavior; expropriation; political instability and conditionality	Gurr (1968) Smith (1971) Knudsen (1974) Chatterjee (1982) Sidell (1988)
2. *Input/Output*	System view of sources, actors and effects of political risk events; nationalism.	Robock (1971) Boddewyn and Cracco (1972)
3. *Product/Market*	Order pattern of industries; bilateral international political relationships; country of origin effects; political climate	Wang (1978) Channon and Jalland (1979) Overholt (1982) Tallman (1988)
4. *Structural*	Structural characteristics of the industry (size, management role, technology, ownership)	Truitt (1970) Knudsen (1974) Jodice (1980) Kobrin (1980) Chapman and Walker (1987) Boddewyn (1988)
5. *Bargaining Power*	Power formation process; shifting perception of benefit/cost ratios; relevant environments; dominance (technology, product differentiation, economies of scale and scope)	Robock (1971) Connor (1977) De la Torre (1981) Farge and Wells (1982) Simon (1984) Root (1990) Jain (1993)
6. *Government Type*	Governmental forms of nation; typology of political models (traditional, pluralistic) and instability.	Behrman (1970, 1971) Vernon (1971) Fayerweather (1973) Green (1974) Brewer (1981, 1983)

Table II:
1987 and 1993 Surveys of Corporate Uses of Political Risk Assessment
(Stapenhurst, 1993)

	1987 Survey (N=18) Mean/Frequency	1993 Survey (N=18) Mean/Frequency	t-stat
1.Number of Analysts	2.2	1.4	.46
2.Other responsibilities (Y/N)	18	18	
3.% of time on Political Risk	46.9%	20.7%	2.19 (a=.10)
4.Use of External Consultants	35%	47.8%	-1.7 (a=.05)
Methodology			
5.Checklisting	5	6	
6.Structured	10	7	
7.Scenario Building	5	5	-1.29
8.Investment Modeling	0	1	
9.Other	1	2	
Process			
10.Ad Hoc	4	7	
11.Regular Studies	7	8	-.1
12.Continuous Assessment	6	4	
13.Other	0	1	
Integration of Assessment into Decision Making Process			
14.Board of Directors	33.3%	29.3%	.54
15.Chairman/President	60.5%	48.8%	1.37
16.Strategic Planning	54.5%	60.0%	.85

Table II (continued):
1987 and 1993 Surveys of Corporate Uses of Political Risk Assessment
(Stapenhurst, 1993)

	1987 Survey (N=18) Mean/Frequency	1993 Survey (N=18) Mean/Frequency	t-stat
Reporting Lines			
17.Board of Directors	0	0	
18.President	4	2	
19.Other Executives	7	10	.85
20.Line Managers	1	1	
21.Staff Managers	6	5	
Location of Assessment Unit			
22.Independent Unit	1	2	
23.Finance Department	0	1	
24.Strategic Planning	4	2	.85
25.Economics Department	4	6	
26.Other	9	7	
Purpose of Risk Evaluations			
27.Investment/Loans Decisions	11	10	
28.Strategic Planning	11	13	
29.Foreign Exchange Operations	5	2	1.47
30.Day to Day Operations	4	2	
31.Other	4	0	
Firm Characteristics			
% with Sales/Loans Overseas	41.1	47.6	-.9
% with Overseas FDI	37.1%	42.9%	-1.3
# of Countries Covered	19.6	18.2	

Discussion of Table II:

Table II compares the surveys conducted in 1987 and 1993 of the political risk assessment activities in multinational corporations. Although there were multiple respondents in both surveys, only 18 companies responded to both the 1987 and 1993 survey. The first section of the table examines the characteristics of the risk assessment group. This includes the number of fulltime analysts, whether the analysts have other non-risk assessment activities, and the percentage of time dedicated to risk assessment. The last figure is the number of external consultants which are employed to do political risk assessment.

The second section of the survey covers the different methodologies employed by the risk assessment groups. The first is the use of simple checklists and the next is the use of more complex structured qualitative formats. The last two are the use of scenarios and investment models. This sub-section is followed by an evaluation of the different processes. Respondents were asked to reply whether monitoring was done on an adhoc, regular periodic, or continuous bases.

The third section of the survey analyzed the integration of the risk assessment into the decision making process, such as who received the information, what were the established reporting lines, location of the risk assessment group, and the purpose of the analysis. Finally, the fourth and last section amassed the characteristics of the respondents.

SOURCES

Agmon, Tamir (1985), *Political Economy and Risk in World Financial Markets*, Lexington, Mass: Lexington Books.

Arbeláez, Harvey (1993), "Political Risk: The First 25 Years, and a Global Public Choice Approach," Presented at Annual Meeting of the Academy of International Business, mimeo.

Ascher, William (1978), *Forecasting: An Appraisal for Policymakers and Planners*, London: John Hopkins Press, pp. 227-239.

Ascher, William (1982), "Political Forecasting," *Journal of Forecasting*, Vol. 1, pp. 137-151.

Ascher, William (1989), "Limits of 'Expert Systems,'" *Technological Forecasting and Social Change*, Vol. 36.

Behrman, Jack (1970), *National Interests and Multinational Enterprise*, Englewood Cliffs: Prentice Hall.

Behrman, Jack (1971), *U.S. International Business and Governments*, Columbia: University of South Carolina Press.

Boddewyn, Jean and Etienne Cracco (1972), "The Political Game in World Business," *Columbia Journal of World Business*, 7, January-February, pp. 45-56.

Boddewyn, Jean (1988), "Political Aspects of MNE Theory," *Journal of International Business Studies*, 19, no. 3, Fall, pp. 341-63.

Brewer, Thomas (1981), "Political Risk Assessment for Foreign Direct Investment," *Columbia Journal of World Business*, Spring, pp. 5-13.

Brewer, Thomas (1983), "Political Sources of Risk in the International Money Markets," *Journal of International Business Studies*, Spring/Summer, pp. 161-164.

Channon, Derek and Michael Jalland (1979), *Multinational Strategic Planning*, London: Macmillan Press.

Chapman, Keith and David Walker (1987), *Industrial Location,* Oxford: Basil Blackwell.

Chatterjee, Asok (1982), *Foreign Direct Investment and Political Risk* Ph.D. dissertation, New York University.

Connor, John (1977), *The Market Power of Multinationals*, New York: Praeger Publishers.

De la Torre, Jose (1981), "Foreign Investment and Economic Development Conflict and Negotiation," *Journal of International Business Studies,* Fall, pp. 9-28.

Farge, Nathan and Louis Wells (1982), "Bargaining Power of Multinational and Host Governments," *Journal of International Business Studies*, Fall, pp. 9-23.

Fayerweather, John (1973), *International Business-Government Affairs*, Cambridge: Bellinger Press.

Friedmann, Roberto and Jonghoon Kim (1988), "Political Risk and International Marketing," *Columbia Journal of World Business*, Winter, pp. 63-74.

Green, Robert (1974), "Political Structures as a Predictor of Radical Political Change," *Columbia Journal of World Business*, Spring, pp. 28-36.

Gurr, Ted (1974), "A Causal Model of Civil Strife," *Columbia Journal of World Business*, 9, December, pp. 29-36.

Haendel, Dan, Gerald West and Robert Meadow (1975), *Overseas Investment and Political Risk*, Philadelphia: The Foreign Policy Research Institute.

Heffernan, Shelagh (1986), *Sovereign Risk Analysis*, London: Allen and Unwim.

Jain, Subhash (1993), *International Marketing Management*, Belmont: Wadsworth Publishing Company.

Jalilvand, A. (1987), "Euromoney and Institutional Investor Country Risk Indices and Predictions of Debt Servicing Problems in Developing Countries," FMA Paper.

Jodice, David (1980), "Sources of Change in Third World Regimes," *International Organization*, 34, Spring, pp. 177-206.

Jones, Randall (1984), "Empirical Models of Political Risks in U.S. Oil Production Operations in Venezuela," *Journal of International Business Studies*, 15 no. 1, pp. 81-95.

Kennedy, Charles (1991), *Managing in the International Business Environment*, Englewood Cliffs, New Jersey: Prentice Hall.

Kennedy, Paul (1987), *The Rise and Fall of the Great Powers*, New York: Random House.

Knudesen, Harald (1992), "Transnational Integration, National Markets and Non-States," Paper presented at a conference on "Perspectives on International Business Theory, Research and Institutional Arrangements" University of South Carolina, May 20-24.

Kobrin, Stephen (1980), "The Assessment and Evaluation of Noneconomic Environment by American Firms," *Journal of International Business Studies*, 11: 32-47.
Overholt, William (1982), *Political Risk*, London: Euromoney Publications.

Purcell, John (1993), *Evaluating Sovereign Credit Risk: A High Yield Analysts Guide*, Salomon Brothers.

Robock, Stephan (1971), "Political Risk: Identification and Assessment," *Columbia Journal of Business,* July/August, pp. 6-20.

Rogers, J. (1992) "Political Risk Analysis," *Risk Management Review,* Spring: 4 no. 7, pp. 4-7.

Root, Franklin (1968), "Attitudes of American Executives in International Business," in A. Kapoor and Philip D. Grub, eds. *The Multinational Enterprise in Transition,* Princeton: Darwin Press, pp. 14-23.

Root, Franklin (1990), *International Trade and Investment*, Cincinnati: South-Western Publishing, Co.

Rummel, R.J. and David Heenan (1978), "How Multinationals Analyze Political Risk," *Harvard Business Review,* January-February, pp. 67-76.

Sethi, S. Prakash and K.A.N Luther (1986), "Political Risk Analysis and Direct Foreign Investment," *California Management Review*, Winter, pp. 57-68.

Sidell, Scott (1988), *The IMF and the Third-World Political Instability,* New York: St. Martin Press.

Simon, Jeffrey (1982), "Political Risk Assessment: Past Trends and Future Prospects," *Columbia Journal of World Business,* Fall, pp. 62-71.

Simon, Jeffrey (1984), "A Theoretical Perspective on Political Risk," *Journal of International Business Studies*, Winter, pp. 123-143.

Smith, Clifford (1971), "Predicting the Political Environment of International Business," *Long Range Planning,* 4, no. 1, pp. 7-14.

Stapenhurst, Frederick (1993), "Political Risk Analysis in North American Multinationals Canadian International Development Agency," mimeo.

Tailman, Stephen (1988), "Home Country Political Risk and Foreign Direct Investment in the United States," *Journal of International Business,* 19, 2, pp. 219-234.

Truitt, J. Frederick (1970), "Expropriation of Foreign Investment," *Journal of International Business Studies,* Fall, pp. 30-35.

Vernon, Raymond (1971), *Sovereignty at Bay,* New York: Basic Books.

Vernon, Raymond (1977), *Storm Over the Multinationals,* Cambridge: Harvard University Press.

Wang, Chih-Kang (1978), "The Effect of Foreign Economic , Political, and Cultural Environment and Consumers' Socio-Demographics on Consumer' Willingness to Buy Foreign Products," Ph.D dissertation, Texas A&M.

World Bank (1992), *World Bank Development Report*, Washington D.C.: World Bank.

SUGGESTED READINGS

Alesina, Alberto and Guido Tabellini (1989), "External Debt, Capital Flight, and Political Risk" *Journal of International Economics*, pp. 199-220.

Ascher, William and W. H. Overholt, *Strategic Planning and Forecasting*, New York: Wiley, 1983.

Ascher, William (1993) "The Ambiguous Nature of Forecasts in Project Evaluation," *International Journal of Forecasting*, pp. 109-115.

Chapter 3

Customizing Risk Analysis
as a Tool for Strategic Management
Sandy Markwick

This paper highlights a distinction between complementary forms of political risk analysis: *country risk* assessment and *project-specific* risk analysis. Having made the distinction the paper argues that companies must integrate both into the decision-making process for political risk management to be fully effective. This is the only way that companies involved in direct investments can ensure an accurate understanding of risk and therefore implement appropriate and effective risk mitigation strategies.

A tendency on the part of global companies to confine the scope of 'political risk' to the provision of 'country risk' analysis fails to bring about comprehensive risk assessments. Too often country risk analysts are relied upon to provide 'political risk' and are separated from business units tasked with drawing up feasibility plans for projects addressing a range of technical and commercial issues.

It is easy to see how, once divorced from the commercial realities in this way, the work of country risk analysts in corporations can then be dismissed as 'ivory tower' exercises of little practical relevance to the commercial realities of a project. Country risk is often tagged on as an introduction or addendum to the core of a feasibility study rather than treated as integral to it.

Meanwhile, project-based political risk analysis, if indeed it is done at all by business units, tends to be removed from the important wider context. Managing political risk is fundamental to the success or otherwise of a project and should be fully integrated along with other technical and commercial issues.

Project risk vs country risk analysis

In practice, the divide between project-specific political risk and country risk is not clearly marked. Instead risks are positioned along a continuum with micro risks at one extreme and *macro* risks at the other (Figure 1). While some risks will be specific to the project itself others may stem from the certain generic characteristics of the project and will be shared with others displaying the same properties. Examples of common characteristics might include type of industry of the project or location in a particular region. Further toward the macro end of the continuum will be a set of risks shared in common with all other direct foreign investors. More macro still, some risks will be shared by all business domestic and foreign.

Generally project-specific risk analysis adds higher value to corporations operating or considering operations around the world than country risk as it highlights the specific risk management strategies required to safeguard a project. Nevertheless, it is also clear that micro risks stemming from specific characteristics of a project must be assessed against a canvass of more general macro risks - those posed by working in a particular environment but which affect all business, or at least broad groups of businesses.

Where companies considering direct investments rely solely on project-specific or generic *country risk* analysis they will have only a partial understanding of the complex risks they will face. Consequently where a company decides to proceed with a project, it may encounter unexpected problems for which managers had not planned or may waste valuable management time on inappropriate strategies. Alternatively, where a company decides *not* to proceed it may be forgoing sound investment opportunities.

Once the differences are appreciated the reasons for the apparent willingness for companies to invest in countries known to be high risk becomes clearer. It is not simply that the commercial opportunities are so attractive that companies are willing to accept high risk. Often, the specifics of a projects and the strategies implemented mean that a project faces lower risks than those generally faced in that country.

For example, oil companies invest in Algeria in spite of the generally high risks associated with government instability and high levels of political violence. Companies run operations far-removed from areas of extremist activity from enclosed compounds in the desert isolation of Hassi Massaoud. With appropriate relationships with the army, foreign oil companies can effectively manage the poor security environment that makes investment in other areas of industry too risky.

Figure 1. Political risk continuum

| | Stakeholder relations | | | Attitudes to foreign investment | | | |
| Terms of contract | | Location | | Industrial sector | | National Origin | Government stability |

Micro project risk   *Macro country risk*

Project variables

No two investments are exactly alike. Among the variables setting investment projects apart are location, industrial sector, national origin of the investor or operator, terms of contract and financial structure. A project's unique characteristics lead to a unique profile of risk exposure. Even two projects sharing many common characteristics may face quite different risks because of one or more key characteristics.

The variable characteristics are diverse, complex and overlapping. The list below is not intended to be comprehensive, but gives a flavour of the types of issues that companies need to consider. In each case the importance of the specific issues is best understood in a wider country risk context.

Industrial sector

Companies that operate some of the 'commanding heights' that are central to an economy – typically the public utilities, transport, heavy industry or banking – generally will face more scrutiny and sensitivity that those in less critical industrial sectors. Foreign investment in infrastructure or natural resources also tends to provoke nationalist sentiment. Country risk analysis completes the picture for a particular investment project by indicating the type and strength of attitudes to foreign investment generally and in relevant sectors in particular, and, by assessing the ability of anti-foreign groups to influence government policy.

Type of investment affecting bargaining power

Other characteristics closely related to the industrial sector of a project will affect a company's bargaining power and therefore its vulnerability to political risk.

Does the company provide capital, technology or expertise that is not available locally? Where a company has negotiated terms of entry with a government, the extent to which a company provides sought-after commodities will affect the balance of power between the two. If a company adds value that is not on offer from local companies there will be a disincentive to the government to interfere to the detriment of the project for fear of chasing away the investors and discouraging other foreign companies from stepping in.

Alternatively, the government may be offering an extremely attractive opportunity for which foreign companies are lining up. When Susuki threatened to pull out of a profitable 15-year joint venture because of a dispute with the Indian government over its choice of a managing director, the Industry Minister challenged the company in no uncertain terms: "there are thousands of people waiting. The Americans are there, there Germans are there...There are several people better than Susuki available in this world."[1]

A large fixed investment may be vulnerable over time to contract renegotiation if it is a large fixed investment that proves successful - a vulnerability known as the 'obsolescing bargain'.[2] A company cannot simply walk away from such an investment, a large power project for example, without simply leaving it to the government to benefit alone from the project's long-term success.

Alternatively, where a project faces domestic competition local interests may provoke nationalist sentiment or use unfair means to present obstacles to foreign participation. In many emerging or Newly Industrialised Countries, there is a growing domestic business sector, particularly in light and medium-industry - less so in the mega-projects which are likely still to require the involvement of international companies. An attempt by British paint manufacturer in 1997 ICI to buy a 9% stake in Asian Paints faced refusal by the government under pressure from Indian industrialists - despite regulations allowing a 51% foreign ownership in the paint industry. Neither was ICI seeking a seat on the board nor management changes. The dispute illustrates the uncertainty that local powerful interests bring to bear on enforcement of apparently clear investment regulations.

Again, country risk will determine the strength of nationalist sentiment and attitudes to foreign participation in the economy. It would also determine the de-

---

[1] Jonathan Karp, "India alarms multinationals," *The Wall Street Journal* (September, 1997).
[2] For a discussion of the 'obsolescing bargain' see Theodore H. Moran, "Introduction: The Growing Role of foreign Direct Investment in the Developing countries" in Theodore H Moran (ed.), *Managing International Political Risk* (Blackwell Business, 1998), pp. 9-12.

gree of domestic competition and the extent to which they would be able to obstruct foreign investment by using unfair advantages to influence weak local state institutions.

Government relations

Does a project have political support? How likely is that support to be durable over time? If this support based on personal or business relationships, how secure are the positions of such 'friends in high places'. If political support is based on synergy between the company and the government's priorities, country risk analysis will be needed to determine the likely prospects for the government's priorities remaining consistent over time.

A good illustration of how political backing can lead to contrasting fortunes among companies with similar profiles can be found in Peru under the left-wing military regime of Gen Juan Velasco in Peru (1968-75). The Velasco government was attempting to modernise the Peruvian economy away from its focus on exports by developing a domestic industrial capacity. The government used the resources of the state to encourage Peruvian business interests over foreign business and the state was given a direct productive role in the economy where domestic business was insufficiently developed.

Foreign mining companies operating in Peru were considered keystones in the traditional export orientated power bloc. Despite rhetoric opposing the activities of foreign mining companies, the government understood that it needed the capital and technical expertise provided by the mining companies to maximise revenues from exports of natural resources for use by the state to further its core priorities. Far from launching an immediate round of nationalisations, the government pursued a rational policy of putting pressure on the mining companies to develop more of their concessions. The failure to reach an agreement over the development of further concessions between the government and US-owned mining companies Marcona Mining and the Cerro de Pasco Corporation led to the expropriation of these companies' entire Peruvian operations. By contrast, the government did not nationalise the Southern Peru Copper Corporation (SPCC) because of the company's commitment to develop its Cuajone copper mine in Southern Peru. The government's approach was not the universal expropriation of all foreign mining companies, but instead it opted to be selective, by allowing companies whose activities were deemed compatible with the government's aims to continue to operate.[3]

Company image

The public image of the company is important. Is the company seen as a tough negotiator that has used its powerful position to squeeze every possible advantage out of the government? Were negotiations conducted behind closed doors opening it up to suspicions of corruption that could be used as political leverage by opposition groups? Or is it considered a fair operator that is operating a project to the mutual benefit of host and company? Is it benefiting the local community? Does it provide employment for local people, not just in terms of numbers but quality too? Is it training locals as managers? Does the company hire local subcontractors? Is the company's environmental record in question?

Any perception that a company's operations are anything other than exemplary may be grist to the mill of local opposition groups attempting to score political points over governing parties.

'Stakeholder' relations

Does the company have an informal 'license to operate' from local communities? Do the benefits of the project outweigh any disadvantages in the eyes of the local community? Is there open dialogue with grass roots and independent groups and Non-Government Organisations (NGO)s that make up the wider civil society outside mainstream channels of power? Genuine community liaison (not public relations exercises) will result in projects that are "demonstrably more acceptable, viable and sustainable."[4]

Poor community relations and social responsibility on the part of investors and operators will invite interference from local or national government. It will also increase political risk of a less traditional nature. The pattern for globalisation in the 1990s has required a broadening of the concept of 'political risk' to include political fallout around the world often led by NGOs to replace narrower definitions focussing on interference by host governments. Intense scrutiny of the

---

[3]For a discussion of the Velasco government's policies towards foreign companies see Rosemary Thorp & Geoffrey Bertram, "Peru 1870-1977: Growth and Policy in an Open Economy." MacMillan 1978.

[4]James Cooney, "Global Mining: three priorities in a politically challenging world," Paper presented to Northwest Mining Association's Annual International Convention, December 1995, Spokane, Washington.

activities of companies, particularly those in natural resources exploitation, has led to rapid appreciation of the issues on the part of some companies and costly damaged reputations for others.

In establishing healthy local community relations it is not sufficient for companies to rely on local political representatives as necessarily representative of local opinion on all issues. This is particularly the case in emerging democracies. A controversy involving GE Capital in Mexico is illustrative of the need to engage wider civil society in discussions about investment projects. The company was part of a consortium to build a hotel, business conference centre and golf course in the town of Tepotzlan. The federal government in Mexico City was behind the project as was the mayor of Tepotzlan, a member of the ruling Institutional Revolutionary Party (PRI). Given this level of local support, the company perhaps could be forgiven for believing it had the support of the local community. Not so. Local residents in the largely farming community were overwhelmingly opposed to the project fearing the diversion of scarce water resources away from local farms. The dispute - soon dubbed the 'Golf War' - lead to persistent unrest over a period of months in 1995 culminating in the death of a protester following which the project was cancelled.

Other risks will stem from the characteristics of the project itself - in the context of the particular investment environment. For example, what is the precise geographic location of the project? Separate gold mining ventures, identical apart from location, will face a different local community of 'stakeholders' - including residents, local landowners and business interests, local political representatives and bureaucracies. As a result the companies will face a unique set of specific risks, requiring unique strategies to manage them.

Local political unrest

Establishing healthy local community relations will be particularly problematic in area separatist, ethnic or political tension. Companies in extractive industries often operate in rural areas where this is the case. If so, is the company seen as neutral or supportive or the central government? What is the nature of the relationship with the security forces?

A deep understanding of the complex dynamics of local political relationships is often required to determine appropriate risk mitigation strategies. For companies in the oil sector working in Nigeria's Delta region, the spate of abductions by local gangs would suggest a need for beefed up security arrangements. Certainly that might be appropriate in the short term. However, closer inspection would suggest also a longer term strategy involving negotiation with central government as well as local groups to help ensure the benefits of oil wealth are distributed locally. There is evidence that abductions - though carried out by gangs of youths are used by local interests to gain political leverage over central government. Effective control of a security problem often requires a political strategy as well as a security strategy. Companies can exert influence to help bring political solutions closer to reality.

BP Amoco's experiences in Colombia illustrate the problems facing companies operating in areas of social conflict. It is widely accepted that the company has gone further than legal required in developing community aid programmes surrounding its drilling sites in the department of Casanare. Significant funds have been directed towards social projects in education, training and the environment and the company has given priority to buying from local companies and employing local people. Royalties of $100m per year go directly to the departmental government.

However, threats from left-wing National Liberation Army (ELN) guerrillas and the activities of right-wing paramilitaries have necessitated extraordinary security measures to protect the company's operations and staff. BP Amoco's relationship with the Colombian military and police has led to accusations that the company is complicit in human rights violations.

Leading Non-government Organisations (NGO)s insist the company should do more to campaign for an improved human rights record in Colombia.[5] NGOs are demanding that companies perform a delicate balancing act: one that uses its influence to the good, but which invites accusations of interfering in the sovereignty of elected governments and neo-colonial arrogance.

Ownership structure

A local joint venture partner is often a useful means to bring aboard a project some useful local knowledge of how business is conducted as well as contacts. Certainly, having a local JV partner may well act as a disincentive to a government to place obstacles in the path of the smooth running of a project. But is can create problems too. Does the local partner have close associations with the government? This may be an advantage in the short term, but in the event of a new government this could prove a disadvantage.

---

[5]Richard Lapper, "Caught in a Cauldron of Guerrilla Violence," *Financial Times* (September 21, 1999).

In the event of a breakdown in the relationship how likely is the former partner to use extra-legal methods or unfair influence on local institutions such as the judiciary to win its claim? Project-specific analysis would determine the extent to which the partner has a reputation for integrity in business dealings and the nature of his/her political associations. Country risk would inform the investor as to the national importance of those connections and also the extent to which powerful interests are able to manipulate local state institutions.

Are there multiple investors behind the project from numerous countries or just one? Are there any difficulties in international relations that could pose a threat to a project because of the national origins of the owners?

A Methodology for Project-Specific Political Risk Analysis

A helpful starting point for a companies undertaking project-based political risk analysis is to appreciate that investments have a political impact. Investments are not neutral and objective conditions superimposed on the local economy and considered universally benign. Instead projects will effect shifts in the balance of power of local relationships. All investments have a socio-economic impact - it is hoped at the very least that they will create employment or earn revenues and create spin off opportunities - and therefore also a *political* impact.

Political impact means direct investments will create 'winners' and 'losers'. At the heart of political risk analysis is identifying the 'winners' and 'losers' and assessing their relative abilities to help or hinder a project. For example, among the list of 'winners' may be new employees, local shops, the project's business partners and local and national public finances. The list of 'losers' might include farming communities and landowners, local residents, competitive business interests or opposition political forces keen to prevent any relationship with foreign capital that might strengthen the government.

The key to political risk management will be devising strategies to create more 'winners' and fewer 'losers' and to lessen the impact on those whose interests continue to be adversely affected by a project. Such risk mitigation strategies will be restricted by the need to maintain the commercial viability of the project.

Prioritising risk

Risk analysis adds most value when it leads to practical solutions for business. Risk on its own is less interesting to corporate managers than the ways to control and minimise it. With this purpose in mind effective risk analysis will breakdown the types of risk according to probability, impact and degree to which it is in the power of the company to manage a risk.

Visual representations are helpful. A simple visual risk analysis might chart the potential impact of a particular risk against its likelihood of occurring. With the x axis representing a continuum from low to high probability and the Y axis representing a continuum from low to high impact. End-users of this analysis can clearly see which areas of risk should take priority in terms of management effort: those with the highest impact or highest probability.

The risks identified as high risk or high probability (a risk identified as both would probably call into question the viability of the project) will be given priority. Where time and resources are scarce, those risks identified as low impact and low probability will most likely be ignored.

Figure 2. Impact-Probability Risk Chart

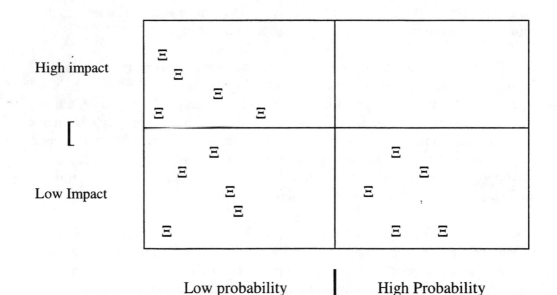

Chapter 4

Managing Project Political Risk*
Gerald T. West - MIGA

Introduction

The work done by a wheelwright and a carpenter differs greatly. Although both work with wood, the latter deals primarily with straight lumber and relatively simple angles; the former deals with curves and compound angles. A wheelwright's chest is filled with specialized tools; even a good carpenter's tool chest looks simple by comparison.

A similar analogy can be made between limited-recourse project developers who have operated solely in their home country and those who have successfully ventured into the developing world. While some of the basic tools and needed skills are similar, it is the specialized tools and the knowledge of how to use them that separate those who are successful in the developing world from those who merely try to apply their home country experience to a new setting.

One of the challenges posed by a prospective limited-recourse project in the developing world is the problem of assessing and managing very different political risks. This article addresses that challenge and describes one of the specialized tools—investment insurance—that can be used to deal with it. Knowing when and how to use political risk investment insurance can allow a project developer to assemble financing for a project that appears to face insurmountable political problems.

Political Risk: Definition and Measurement

More than twenty years ago, I wrote that there was a great deal of semantic and conceptual confusion surrounding the analysis and management of political risk.[1] I still believe that is true today.

---

* This chapter originally appeared as Gerald T. West, "Managing Project Political Risk: The Role of Investment Insurance," *The Journal of Project Finance*, Vol. 2 No. 4 (Winter 1996), pp. 5-11. It is reprinted here with permission from Institutional Investor Systems, Inc.

Because the term "political risk" is often used in a general fashion, it is common to find that different individuals in the same firm have a different understanding of exactly what risks that term encompasses (or excludes). When multiple firms (perhaps from different countries) gather their financiers, lawyers, and accountants together to discuss political risk, confusion is the norm. Considerable time is usually spent exchanging views of what is (or is not) included under the umbrella label "political risk." It is not unusual for the term to be temporarily abandoned, as participants considering a prospective limited-recourse project find it more useful to talk about the specific "risk of loss due to A, B, or C" rather than presume everyone has a common understanding of political risk.

Notwithstanding the conceptual confusion that often surrounds it, however, it is useful to make some general observations.

Political risk is commonly referred to as corporate exposure to risk as a result of politically and socially generated change. Political risks are usually distinguished from conventional economic risks that arise from uncertainties relating to future changes in cost, demand, and competition in the marketplace. Risks that do not fall into the latter category (apart from insurable casualty risks, such as fire and theft) are generally considered political risks by many investors.

In practice, economic and political risks are often difficult to differentiate. The intimate government involvement in national economies frequently obscures whether changes in cost, competition, or demand result from economic or political forces. For an investor, whether risk has political or economic roots is often of lesser importance; the investor must be concerned with the complete set of factors that may affect a prospective investment.

Political and economic risk is often distinguished according to the investor's perception of the proximate cause of the risk. Pragmatically, a risk is often perceived to be political if it relates to:

1. A potential government act (law, decree, regulation, administrative decision, etc.)
2. General instability in the political/social system (war, strife, frequent changes in government, etc.)

For most purposes, a simple definition of political risk will suffice: Political risk is the probability of the occurrence of some political event that will change the prospects for the profitability of a given investment.

Exposure to a political event is usually defined as the maximum amount that an investor would lose if a given event occurred. The critical focal point in political risk assessment and management should be the investor and the specific investment. Beginning with the initial step of identifying and measuring one's exposure to various political risks in successive time periods, the objectives and uniqueness of each individual investor should largely determine how one assesses risk and seeks to manage it.

It is important to note that risk is not a quality inherent in a country, a government, or an environment; risk is a property associated with an individual investor and prospective investment. What represents an unacceptable risk to one investor may be simply a routine manageable situation for another. The management style in one firm may dictate that nearly all variables affecting a potential investment need to be controlled with a high degree of certainty; management in another firm may be willing to venture forth in the face of high risk and many unknowns. Only the firm itself can decide what risk is relevant to it, what degree of risk is acceptable, and how to manage the risk it faces.

For limited-recourse investors, in particular, it is important that their individual approach to the measurement and assessment of political risk remain focused on the project and not on the country. The interests of the different participants in a limited-recourse project will vary with the nature of their asset exposure to different kinds of political risk. Long-term debt investors face slightly different political risks than short-term debt investors; the risks faced by contractors, suppliers, and equity investors will also vary.

All parties, however, need to avoid the temptation to abandon the individual task of analyzing the risks they face. It is tempting to avoid the apparent complexity of political risk as it applies to the individual investor in favor of some holistic risk assessment focused on the country. The "country risk ratings" prepared by various publications and consultant groups are somewhat seductive in their appeal, but very questionable in their methodology. After all, they generally purport to evaluate and measure all the important political and socioeconomic factors affecting an investor, and reduce them to convenient number or letter grade. While some of these services do distinguish between short-term versus long-term risk, trade exposure versus investment exposure, economic versus political risk, and different sectors, most of these services implicitly, if not explicitly, promote the concept that they serve the needs of all investors. Their relevance to any particular investor is thus obviously low.

The Management of Political Risks

While techniques to analyze the political risks facing large-scale projects have improved over the last decade, their integration with a project's financial and economic risk analyses has always been difficult. Like all risk, political risk can be managed once it has been identified and assessed. It must be acknowledged, however, that there are fewer mechanisms available to project developers in managing political risks than in dealing with other types of risk. The astute project developer knows that the key challenge he faces in assembling financing for a project is to devise a division of risks and rewards that is acceptable to each of the interested parties today, and which provides comfort to them that the likely future division of risks and rewards will also be acceptable.

When the political risk analysis of a prospective project is completed, it is possible that the risk is simply so significant that there is little doubt the project should be abandoned. At the opposite extreme, the analysis could reveal that the risk is so minimal that one or more parties are willing to bear (retain) the risk of a loss due to political causes. Obviously, most political risk analyses yield results that fall within those two extremes, and the project developer needs to deal with the challenge of devising a division of the risks among various parties.

Like other kinds of catastrophic risks, every party is usually eager for someone else to bear the primary burden of the risk of a total expropriation without compensation. Even if the risk of such a catastrophe is deemed remote, some party nevertheless needs to bear it. Each participant is often eager that it be someone else, and, because the risk of loss is so unlikely, most would agree that the bearer should only receive a "minor financial consideration" for such a risk assumption. Needless to say, the prospective bearer of such a risk often has a different opinion as to the reward that should be received. In sum, pricing is often a matter of concern among the interested parties.

In broad terms, where a political risk analysis reveals that the prospective project should not be abandoned or that all the risks simply should be borne by the sponsors, there are three risk management strategies that project developers can pursue: transfer, risk minimization and loss prevention, and insurance. The astute project developer knows that the selection of one of these strategies (or a combination) should flow from the nature and specifics of each project—allowing for different investors' goals and expectations and their respective corporate cultures. The project developer's goal is clearly to select a strategy (or a hybrid of them) that attracts the needed partners and who, in turn, are comfortable with the risk they are asked to assume and the rewards they anticipate reaping.

A brief word about each of the strategies is useful. By transfer, we refer to the sharing of equity ownership of a prospective investment with other foreign investors, project financiers, and local interests in the host country. The goal of this equity sharing is not merely to proportionately reduce the firm's exposure to certain political risks, but through the astute selection of partners, to reduce the political risk in an amount disproportionate to the amount of ownership relinquished. Project developers, in some circumstances, need to be prepared to partially push aside purely financial considerations and select partners on the basis of their political "clout." Especially valuable partners in some countries are local investors who are "above" the political fray, honest, and are not closely identified with one political party or faction.

By risk minimization and loss prevention, we refer to an array of techniques that attempt to either reduce the amount of assets at risk or to minimize the incidence of a loss. In the former case, a number of purely financial techniques (e.g., currency swaps, payment leads and lags, etc.) can serve to marginally reduce the amount an investor has at risk at any one time. After analysis of a particular situation, specific cost-effective, risk-minimization techniques can be matched to the risk exposure. In the category of loss prevention, various public and community relations programs are often an excellent prophylactic against local political problems.

Management ingenuity can often solve very specific micro-political problems. For example, subsequent to attempted shakedowns by corrupt customs officials, significant delays, and regular pilferage of equipment in a West African port, one investor packaged all his remaining project equipment and goods on one ship. As it arrived in port, a popular local musician visited the quay and promised the port's entire stevedore crew free tickets to a special concert, beer, and T-shirts if the ship was unloaded and the goods were delivered to the investor in two days. Everything was delivered on time with no pilferage whatsoever, as custom officials dared not delay the possibility of such a reward.

By insurance, we refer to the transfer of the risk of loss due to specified political perils to an insurance entity. Insurance coverage can be selectively purchased to cover some, but not all, investors; if desired, insurance may cover only certain portions of the project or certain financial instruments. Insurance obviously can help establish the pricing of risk within a project and thus facilitate its sharing among other interested parties. As will be noted subsequently, the political risk investment insurance market is quite unusual in that there are three groups of insurers active in the market: national agencies, private-sector underwriters, and multilateral entities. Each group exists for different purposes and has different capabilities; hence, there are different costs and benefits associated with using each of them. This can work to the advantage of a savvy investor or project developer.

The Investment Insurance Market

More than twenty countries, primarily Organization for Economic Cooperation and Development (OECD) countries, have established agencies or programs to promote international investment by their own nationals. In some countries, a single agency promotes both trade and investment through insurance and finance programs (e.g., the Export Credits Guarantee Department (ECGD) in the U.K., and Compagnie Francaise d'Assurance pour le Commerce Exterieur (COFACE) in France). In others, separate agencies have been created (e.g., in the U.S., the Overseas Private Investment Corporation (OPIC) for investments and Eximbank for trade transactions).

By far the largest investment insurance programs are those established by Japan Export/Import Insurance Department/Ministry of International Trade and Industry (EID/MITI), the U. S. (OPIC), and Germany (TREUARBEIT); the programs of the U.K., France, and Canada are also significant. These programs offer long-term coverage relatively quickly (several months) and at reasonable premiums. However, they often have somewhat narrow and changeable eligibility criteria.

A small group of private insurers have also developed political risk coverage for private investors. The major firms in this market today are Lloyd's of London, American International Underwriters (AIU), Citicorp International Trade Indemnity (CITI), and Unistat Assurance.

In comparison with the national schemes that provide long-term, noncancelable coverage for fifteen to twenty years (because they are backed by their governments), private insurers can usually offer coverage from only one to three years (although recently some private insurers have started to offer up to seven years in coverage). While national insurers have premium rates in a relatively narrow range, private insurers' rates can fluctuate widely based on supply and demand, as well as their risk analyses. Private insurers offer great flexibility in structuring coverage and quick response time, but they are often unable to provide currency transfer and political violence coverage in many developing countries and emerging economies.

A number of multilateral organizations have created risk transfer mechanisms of various kinds: 1) the World Bank (IBRD) has a guarantee program that can protect lenders against payment defaults. These guarantees have supported private borrowings for public-sector entities and can also be used to support private-sector projects; 2) the Inter-American Development Bank has completed its design of a program very similar to the IBRD's guarantee program; and 3) regional programs such as the Inter-Arab Investment Guarantee Agency are also available for selected projects.

By far the largest of these multilateral programs is the Multilateral Investment Guarantee Agency (MIGA). Established in 1988 with capital of $1 billion and a member of the World Bank Group, MIGA was created to fill gaps in the availability of political risk coverage for foreign investment in developing countries and emerging markets. MIGA's advantage in the marketplace stems from its unique ownership structure (currently 138 member countries), and its ability to provide coverage to investors from all its member countries.

The national insurers and MIGA can generally insure investments in either new projects or in the expansion, modernization, privatization, or financial restructuring of existing projects. These agencies are flexible and generally able to cover different forms of investment: equity, shareholder loans, shareholder loan guarantees, technical assistance, and management contracts. Financial institutions are usually eligible to pursue insurance for their own investments and for project loans. Coverage can typically be provided against expropriation, currency transfer, and political violence (war, revolution, insurrection, civil strife, etc.).

Perhaps the most important development in the investment insurance marketplace in recent years is the increasing collaboration among investment insurers in light of the high demand to cover large multinational projects, especially infrastructure projects. It is increasingly common that multiple insurers are offering coverages on the same large project.

Coverage by multilateral organizations such as MIGA serves to enhance the utility of investment insurance as a risk management tool, because it not only expands available insurance capacity through the institution's own underwriting, but enhances the capabilities of the whole industry through reinsurance and coinsurance activities.

MIGA, for example, has a mandate to complement other underwriters (both private and public) in the promotion of investment into developing countries. It has signed project reinsurance arrangements with Canadian, Japanese, and U.S. national agencies, as well as a private reinsurer, and is participating in coinsurance arrangements with a large number of private and public insurers. Such collaboration with other insurers effectively increases the available insurance capacity for all international investors.

Investment Insurance: The Quiet Facilitator

Investment insurance has been rightly termed the "quiet facilitator" of limited-recourse private investment in the developing world for several reasons. The first is secrecy about its existence and underestimation of its value.

It is a condition of almost all private investment insurance policies that the existence of the policy not be revealed. If it is revealed and there is a claim, the insurer has a sound legal basis for denying payment of the claim. Hence, millions of dollars in premiums are quietly paid to private insurers and many claims are quietly settled. This silence about political risk investment insurance is also reflected in academia and in the media; there is little attention paid to it.

A different kind of secrecy exists among the about twenty national (public) insurers. While a few of these insurers notify both the public and host country of the existence of an investment insurance policy, most national insurers do neither. Hence, the fact that firms purchase billions of dollars of coverage annually from national insurers goes largely unnoticed by investors, academicians, and the media.

Another reason why investment insurers are underappreciated as facilitators of investments concerns their role in the settlement of investment disputes and claims. Few investment insurers make public their claims payments. Moreover, very little is ever said or written about an insurer's role in the resolution of investment disputes. At one large national insurer, only one of four notifications of a potential claim by an insured investor actually resulted in a claims payment. The other three were quietly resolved before they resulted in a loss.

Why is little said or written about this phenomenon? One might answer that question with a question: What national investment insurer from an OECD country wishes it known that it has convinced, cajoled, pressured, induced, persuaded, or otherwise reasoned with a developing country, so that a specific investment was not expropriated? No one. For similar reasons, it is not in the interest of the investor who has benefited from such a dispute resolution to publicize it. Silence about such events obviously makes good business sense for an investor who wishes to continue to operate.

The host country, in turn, is not eager to publicize the resolution of a conflict or dispute with foreign investors for two reasons. First, it is difficult for most governments to admit publicly that a reversal of government decision or action has taken place; and second, they are often afraid to undermine the government's credibility and their country's image of being an attractive investment site.

Together, these two phenomena (i.e., investment insurance secrecy and its role in the settlement of investment disputes and claims) have had the interesting effect of making some investors who have benefited from interventions by investment insurers staunch "believers" and users of investment insurance. Conversely, other firms who have viewed such insurance solely in terms of compensation for a possible loss and never seriously evaluated insurance in terms of its deterrence value, often cannot understand why investment insurance is so highly valued by others. Needless to say, such firms tend to never seriously look at investment insurance - much less purchase it. There is an important, but subtle, difference between private and public political risk insurers. If both groups were property insurers, it could be said that one group installs lightning rods (i.e., provides service to mitigate the effects of a loss) and the other both installs lightning rods and seeks to influence the weather (i.e., to reduce the frequency of lightning strikes on the building).[2]

Investors' demand for political risk insurance from private, national, and multilateral agencies has grown rapidly. The Berne Union, comprising twenty-two national investment insurers (and MIGA), reported a significant increase in coverage issued, from $2.3 billion in 1989 to over $8 billion in 1995. When published, their 1996 results should also report a substantial growth in coverage. For example, MIGA increased the number of contracts signed in FY96 by 18% over FY95, and the amount of coverage issued by 28%.

Investment Insurance and Project Finance

In the developing world, a characteristic of large prospective projects, especially in the infrastructure area, is that there is an abundance of risk—technical, economic, business, and political. Even experienced project developers find that the aggregate risk associated with the majority of these prospective deals is prohibitive. In the iterative process of reviewing many prospective projects, the broad technical, economic, and political character of a project needs be sound initially before proceeding with a costly in-depth analysis. Subsequent to establishing the basic technical and economic soundness of a project through an in-depth analysis, a developer's attention usually turns to identifying potential partners and securing project financing.

Astute project developers have been quick to recognize that investment insurance is uniquely able, in some circumstances, to facilitate the assembly of project financing. Because investors from OECD countries normally rely heavily on long-term debt capital to finance large projects, especially private infrastructure projects, securing long-term debt financing is often critical. To provide it, lenders need to know who is bearing what risks—including the political risks. A project developer should know how to tap and use investment insurance schemes to selectively satisfy the political risk transfer needs of long-term lenders.

Investment insurance has proven to be an important mechanism for facilitating limited recourse projects. It is particularly useful because it helps to both mitigate investors' fears and clarify the division of who is bearing what risks. The investment insurance industry has also demonstrated a willingness and an ability to work with investors in putting together the financing for projects. This can be briefly illustrated by describing a power project MIGA assisted in Honduras in 1994.

The ELCOSA project involved the development of a 60mw electric power facility located near the port of Puerto Cortes in Honduras; it became the first private power project in the country. The project developer was Wartsila Diesel Development Corporation, Inc. (WDD).

The core financial problem was that WDD needed to secure financing (both equity and debt) for the project enterprise—Electricidad de Cortes S.R.L. de C.J. (ELCOSA), a special-purpose company formed in partnership with a group of Honduran industrialists. At the same time, WDD was trying to negotiate the sale to two other investors of 51% of the project enterprise. In addition, due to the economic conditions in Honduras (including the delay in signing an RAF agreement with the Honduran government), the national Dutch insurer was hesitant to offer coverage to two Dutch banks for their loans to the project. Wartsila wanted a flexible investment insurance policy in order to attract both equity and debt financing.

MIGA worked actively with other bilateral and multilateral institutions, including the IFC, to facilitate financing for this project. MIGA quickly issued a guarantee to WDD for U.S. $27 million against the risks of currency transfer, expropriation, war, and civil disturbance. At the same time, MIGA issued a U.S. $23 million commitment letter to WDD, providing them with the option to purchase additional coverage. To facilitate the final structuring of the project's financing, MIGA's guarantee and the commitment letter provided Wartsila the option to transfer coverage to other unknown but eligible equity and debt investors in the project enterprise (ELCOSA).

Subsequently, Wartsila transferred equity and debt coverages to four other investors. The first such transaction resulted in the transfer of $4 million equity coverage to Illinova Generating Company, and $5.9 million to the Scudder Latin American Trust for Independent Power. WDD retained coverage of $1.9 million for its 10% equity stake in ELCOSA. In separate $9 million guarantee contracts, MIGA coverage was also extended to two Dutch banks (ING Bank and Mees Pierson) for their loans of $10 million each to the project.

As a result, MIGA issued a total of five contracts for the ELCOSA project—three to equity investors totaling U.S. $12 million (covering WDD, Scudder Latin American Trust for Independent Power, and Illinova Generating Company), and two contracts totaling U.S. $18 million to ING Bank and Mees Pierson.

MIGA's flexible offer of coverage to various participants in advance of their identification was instrumental in the assembly of the project's final financing, as it was a *sine qua non* for the involvement of two Dutch banks. Both the investors and MIGA were very satisfied with the results of this mechanism and it was essentially duplicated for a larger private power project Wartsila developed in Jamaica in 1996.

GERALD T. WEST is a senior advisor at MIGA Guarantees in Washington, DC.

ENDNOTES

[1] See Dan Haendel, and Gerald West. "Overseas Investment and Political Risk." Monograph Number 21, Philadelphia, Foreign Policy Research Institute, 1975.

[2] The author is indebted to Curtis McDonald for this metaphor.

Chapter 5

The Application of Classical Risk Assessment Methodology to Political Risk Assessment

Dr. C.W.J. Bradley & Dr. Michael K. O'Leary

ABSTRACT

Recent events have dramatised the importance and difficulty of political risk assessment for foreign direct investment decision making. Surveys of management personnel and more subjective reports in the literature indicate long-standing and wide-spread recognition of the significance of political risks, yet frequently the assessment of political risk is not very carefully or rigorous undertaken. This paper parallels the well-established methodology utilises for risk assessment within the engineering industry and proposes methodology within the arena of political risk assessment.

The paper introduces a computer program jointly developed by DBA Risk Management and Political Risk Services as part of their effort to integrate the assessment of political risks with the assessment of technical and financial risks in business operations.

§ § §

INTRODUCTION

THE ENGINEERING PERSPECTIVE

Following numerous major disasters over the last 20 years such as Flixborough, Bhopal and Piper Alpha, extensive industrial and government resources have been concentrated on the development of methods for the identification and assessment of major hazards. A wide range of computer software has been developed for the prediction of damage from fires, missiles and explosions as well as for the dispersion of toxic and flammable releases.

Although not a precise science increasingly governments demand a formalised methodology for the assessment of risks within major industrial processes. Many national legislative bodies throughout the industrial world now require detailed risk assessments to be carried out as proof of safe operation.

Formal technical risk assessment enables hazards to be identified and investigated in a systematic way. The likely causes of incidents with the potential to cause accidents can be determined and probability of major accidents estimated. Knowledge of the probability of undesirable events together with the extent of the consequences enables the risk to be determined. The output from formal Quantitative Risk Assessment may then be used for comparative purposes between similar installations and/or setting standards or making commercial decisions.

THE COMMERCIAL PERSPECTIVE

From a commercial point of view risk can be subdivided into two categories as follows:

- Speculative Risks.
- Risks of Loss. (Non-speculative risks.)

Speculative risks cover the loss of a firm's assets from such mainstream business activities as marketing, sales, investment, and production. Although substantial losses can occur in these operations from such unfavourable developments as exchange rate changes, inflation, and new government regulations, such considerations are not typically covered by insurance protection.

In contrast, non-speculative risks, the type covered by insurance protection, encompass only events which result in a loss to a firm and which arise from some observable act of omission where either the cause or the effect is particular to the firm or the individual.

Despite many differences in detail, both engineering and commercial risk management are concerned with preserving the firm's assets from random undesirable events. Furthermore, both involve the classic options regarding risk: to transfer it, to eliminate it, or to accept it. Their aims correspond to the general purposes of an enterprise's risk management: to contribute towards achievement of the firm's objectives.

Political risk assessment may be defined as the systematic means of assessing and managing the political risks of foreign direct investment or international business. Although there are many different definitions of political risk, most agree that it refers to the legal and social environment in which a firm must operate. The purpose of political risk assessment may be defined as:

- A means to identify those elements of political risk associated with foreign direct investment, i.e. identify those countries which have the potential to become the Bosnia, Libya, and Algeria of tomorrow so as to provide sufficient warning to allow a firm time to protect itself or to minimise its exposures.
- A means to identify those countries which have been unnecessarily discounted for political risks or where the political risk of foreign direct investment has decreased.
- A means to compare those countries where political risk is significant but not high enough to automatically rule them out.
- A means for providing information to business decision-makers to assist them in deciding whether to transfer risk, to provide defences against it, or to accept it.

In the engineering industry the acronym ALARP refers to a risk being "As Low As Reasonably Practicable"; the aim of political risk assessment is to strive to define an equivalent situation.

THE ROLE OF THE RISK MANAGER

The role of the risk manager in a corporate structure is usually defined as the task of identifying the risks to which an organisation is exposed, followed by the measurement and development of appropriate methods for handling them.

The role extends not only to the need to explore the possible ways of reducing the uncertainties associated with a particular activity but also explore methods of reducing the costs of these events. The expected costs can be evaluated as a function of both the cost and the probability of the loss event to the company as follows:

$$E = C \times P$$

Where:

E= the expected cost to the company
C= cost of loss
P= the probability of the loss

Thus by reducing either the probability of the loss event or its impact on the company, the expected cost can be reduced. Of course, technical or commercial loss prevention is not loss free; one task of the risk manager is to propose the criteria by which loss prevention can be evaluated. Effective fulfilling of this role involves the measurement of the probability and consequences of undesirable events. This is why a systematic rational for political risk assessment is required.

In a large organisation, the risk manager is a senior part of the management team. In smaller companies, the role is combined with that of the Managing Director. In both cases, the job implies the combined responsibilities for maximising the commercial objectives set for the whole organisation subject to various constraints.

Corporate objective may be defined as:
- Survival of the Company.
- Profit Maximisation.
- Sales Maximisation.
- Increase Shareholders Wealth and Earnings.
- Public Legal Objectives
- Social Objectives (Good Public Relations).

Typical commercial constraints include:
- Statutory Requirements.
- Contractual Conditions.
- Borrowing Constraints.

This description of the risk management function defines a wide area of potential responsibility. The responsibilities of a particular risk manager will depend upon individual company. Many of the available tools for the assessment of potential risks are common to both engineering and risk management disciplines.

In general, the process of risk management and engineering risk assessment may be combined into a single integrated process as follows:

- Identification of the risks to which the organisation is exposed.
- Evaluation of the risks to which the organisation is exposed.
- Control of the risks.

When political risk assessment is considered the three steps though similar to, engineering and insurance risk assessment may be expressed slightly differently as follows:

- Identification of those elements of political risk associated with a foreign investment and to develop an intelligence system to monitor and evaluate changing political conditions within the host country.

- To enable a firm to respond to changing conditions of political risk by integrating the political risk assessment with the firms strategic planning.

- To devise strategies to protect the firm from risk, ranging from persistent risks imposing moderate costs to the less likely but devastating risks such as physical attacks or expropriation.

Business executives sometimes consider that the tools readily available to the engineer are deemed too complex or inappropriate in considering political risk. It estimating the desirability of employing systematic methods, however, it should be kept in mind that the current mainstream methodologies and analytical tools used in engineering risk assessment have been slowly developed and refined over the last 20 years. The development of these tools in the early days required overcoming substantial scepticism as to the efficacy of such a systematic approach.

The now well-defined process of technical risk assessment was once characterised by unclear definitions of the key events that contribute to loss, weak mathematical tools for the assessment of the probability of an undesirable event, and inadequate theoretical understanding of the consequences. In the 1970s engineering risk assessment was largely subjective, heavily dependent upon arbitrary checklists, making use of ranking scales that attempted to weigh the key issues contributing to the potential risk within an installation or plant. Since then, both the available tools and methods have been refined into internationally accepted approaches, resulting in growing confidence in the results obtained from engineering risk assessment.

HOLISTIC RISK MANAGEMENT Methodology & Assumptions

Although this paper presents an outline of how we use the tools already commonplace within the engineering industry to assess political risk, we are increasing required by clients to assess all potential project management, operational, investment, political and environmental risk for safety/environmental, insurance and investments purposes. We refer to this process as Holistic Risk Management (HRM), as opposed to the traditionally piecemeal approach undertaken by most company departments and industries. HRM treats all risks in the same fashion by division of the risk assessment process into two discrete activities:

- Quantification of the likelihood that a potential hazard will occur.
- Assessment of the consequences – the level of impact resulting from the identified hazard.

The classical quantitative risk assessment (QRA) process itself may be subdivided into five steps as shown in Figure 1. These may be defined as Hazard (or Failure Case) Identification, Failure Frequency Estimation, Consequence Modelling, Risk Calculations and Risk Assessment.

Figure 1: The Risk Management Process

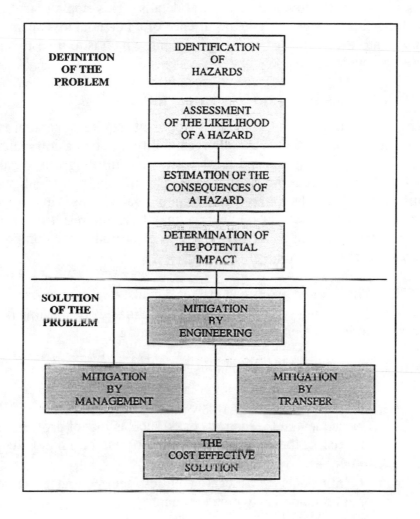

ACTIVITY 1: IDENTIFICATION OF INVESTMENT/PROJECT FRAME WORK AND CASH FLOWS

The first stage of political risk assessment is to subdivide the proposed or on-going project into manageable sections. This is usually achieved by consideration of the overall project time-line in some systematic forms such as a Gantt Chart and associated cash flow and investment details. This step allows the assessment of the financial damage from the occurrence of a potential loss scenario. It acts as the input into the next stage of the assessment, which is to investigate the linkage between an event and its potential consequence.

ACTIVITY 2: LOSS SCENARIO IDENTIFICATION

The risk manager in a technical environment requires a general knowledge of the relevant technical details as well as an ability to retain a commercial overview of the company's financial and legal position. Fulfilling this requirement provides confidence that a proper judgement can be made to identify hazards and quantify the major risks to the overall commercial activity. In many cases a risk with apparently little technical relevance may have the result of inflicting severe damage to the share capital or even result in bankrupting the company. Two approaches are often followed:

- Checking of assets and markets against exposure to risk.
- Classifying risks under various headings. The various possible exposures are then listed under each heading.

A typical classification list might include the following:

- Direct risk revolution, terrorism, theft, war, kidnap.
- Consequential (or indirect) risks, such as loss of profits following a direct risk at the company's premises or that of a major supplier or customer.
- Social risks, such as legal liabilities incurred under statute of contract or at common law within the country.
- Policy-related risks, such as the acts of the home or foreign governments.
- Financial risks, such as inadequate financial forecasting especially of key factors such as economic growth, inflation, or consumer demand.

Making judgements based on an individual bases of perceived risk or by the use of simple checklists presents a major danger: the criteria may change from one assessor to another or from one time period to another as opinion change. This is why making use of a systematic risk assessment protocol (containing defined and agreed rule sets) enables reproducible comparisons to be made between one system or investment and another.

Prior to any assessment the company risk manager must establish full details of the activities of the organisation and identify its assets. It is therefore necessary to undertake a complete survey of all activities, locations and markets in which the company operates and use a methodology, which can be used to compare one risk, one process or one investment with another.

ENGINEERING HAZARD IDENTIFICATION

Within the sphere of engineering risk assessment there has been much written regarding the distinction between risk and hazard. The two terms are defined below.

HAZARD. Hazards are defined as the potential for harm or damage to people, property, environment or the corporate structure. Hazards include the characteristics of things and the actions or inaction of people.

Risk. Risk is a measure of the probability and severity of an adverse effect. The engineering methodology for the formal assessment of risk involves an answer (more or less precise) of three questions: 1) What failure events are likely to occur? 2) What is their expected frequency? 3) What are the likely damages and costs that will result from these failures? One definition of risk is:

$$R = F \times D \times P$$

Where
$$R = \text{Risk}$$
$$F = \text{Number of failures expected in a given time}$$
$$D = \text{Damage resulting from these failures}$$
$$P = \text{Perceived risk}$$

This forms the framework for comprehensive engineering risk assessments, which are broken down into a number of discrete auditable stages.

These definitions represent more that an academic nicety. One failure of risk assessment is that the assessor may make an intuitive judgement as to both the likelihood and severity of the issue too early in the analysis process. In such a case hazards may be identified without first undertaking a full assessment on the basis of the installed protection or a low probability.

As an example consider the case of a fast turning component of an engine within a factory. Is there a hazard or a risk present if a metal guard protects the flywheel? If the assessor follows risk identification rational, then the issue is ignored as there is protection in place; on the other hand, if the assessor follows the procedure for hazard identification, the dangerous situation is identified. In the case of the motor flywheel example this is a vital distinction as the hazard is present whether or not there is protection. Under certain conditions, for example during maintenance when the guard is removed the operator may well be exposed to the hazard.

This notion has significant application to the identification of political risk, because many political risk assessments are captivated by such "headline" events as tumultuous political events, violent attacks on people and property, massive financial disturbances, or expropriation of assets.

This approach raises the prospect of several potentially quite heavy costs by twisting business decisions into either of two contrasting distortions. On the one hand, the focus on the dramatic and traumatic may discourage the business from pursuing a potentially lucrative opportunity. On the other hand, the approach may lead to an ignoring of a wide range of less prominent, but quite damaging, risks arising from less dramatic actions by government and other groups within the operating environment. In short, the approach opens the assessor to the danger of excluding free ranging thought and hindering the timely identification of critical issues. The political risk assessor should therefore attempt to identify political hazards rather than political risks as the starting point of the analysis.

The engineering industry has attempted to address this danger by involving multidisciplinary teams for hazard identification. This is most commonly done by the use of a technique referred to as a Hazard & Operability Study (HAZOP). HAZOP involves bringing together a group of individuals from differing academic and practical backgrounds to analyse a design. Their goal is to identify potential hazards within a system under different operation conditions. It is a precursor to further analysis to determine both the probability and consequences from the identified hazard.

The technique hinges on the assumption that a problem will occur only as a result of deviations from the norm. The methodology is strictly applied by a chairman and recorded by a technical secretary utilising a list of guidewords and a series of potential deviations from the norm. It is in effect a structured brainstorming exercise which asks the question "What if...." and, "So What...." at each stage of an integrated system. The purpose of the multidisciplinary team is to maximise the chance that potential discipline interfaces are identified as well as providing a broad technical base for problem solving during the exercise.

POLITICAL HAZARD IDENTIFICATION

We are expanding the engineering approach to hazard identification, the HAZOP, to include rigorous political hazard identification. In the case of conventional HAZOP, the practitioner systematically addresses the logical flow of materials through process items of equipment as the reference points. Expanding the technique to encompass political risk also involves examining a project's main political steps, commercial actions, and management milestones, as follows:

- Obtain a full description of the intended investment including time scales, economic assumptions, and public policy expectations.
- Subdivide the decision making process into a series of discrete stages.
- Appoint a Political Hazard Identification officer and secretary.
- Form a team with a maximum size of six persons.
- Define a series of guidewords and deviations.
- Apply the guidewords in a consistent manner to each stage of the activity to systematically investigate the potential for political hazards to exist under different conditions.
- Record the results the results.

In the case of political risk the following categories are subdivided into:

- Macro political risk considerations
- Micro political risk considerations

Each of these can be further divided into three additional subcategories: internal government, external government, and society. As an example a list of guidewords for an internal, governmental-related macro political risk might include the following:

- Nationalisation
- Expropriation
- Creeping nationalisation
- Repatriation restrictions
- Leadership struggle

- Radical regime change
- Inflation
- Interest Rates
- Bureaucratic interference.

ACTIVITY 3: FREQUENCY ANALYSIS

This activity that is part of a risk assessment requires the frequency of individual loss scenarios to be estimated. Such an estimate is usually undertaken by the use of a combination of approaches, which include analysis of historical data, political databases and expert judgement based on experience

Even though extensive actuarial statistics have been collected since the 1970s within the engineering industry, much of the input data is still subjective. Wide use is made of the Delphi method (systematic surveys of specialists) and various industrial databases. Hence there has been much argument within the engineering industry as to the validity of probabilistic assessment as well as the accuracy or otherwise of the input data used to predict individual events. Nevertheless it is generally accepted that the main value of statistical methods lies not in the absolute number generated but rather as tools for comparison between alternative designs or alternative decisions. Although the same concerns apply with respect to political risk assessment, formalised risk assessment with a defined methodology enables the sensitivities of various assumptions to be tested and points to areas where further research is needed.

ACTIVITY 4: SCENARIO DEVELOPMENT

Once the type of risk of interest has been identified and appropriate data has been collected the next step is to specify the potential sources of those risks and the logic of how various events and sub-events can lead to the final outcome. For example government instability in a developing countries is one source of risk. But such instability is not the only one; in fact, in many cases it may not be the most important one for many business decisions. It is therefor necessary to undertake a more encompassing analysis of the political sources of risk that addresses the complete array of the events that can lead to threats and damage to a business project.

Event Tree Analysis is an especially useful method that has been adapted from engineering analysis to model the most likely outcome from various permutations and combinations of initiating events.

EVENT TREE ANALYSIS

Event tree analysis is used within the engineering industry to evaluate potential accident that might result following an equipment failure or process upset. It is a "forward thinking" process. Event trees are a modified form of decision trees, which are widely used in business applications. Event trees provide a precise way of recording the sequence of a loss event and defining the relationships between the initiating events and the subsequent events that combine to result in a loss. Then by ranking the loss events, or through a subsequent quantitative evaluation, the most important loss event may be identified.

Event trees are well suited for analysing initiating events that could result in a variety of effects. An event tree emphasises the initial cause and works from the initiating event to the final effects of the event. Each branch of the event tree represents a separate effect (event sequence) that is a clearly defined set of functional relationships.

The analysis begins with an initiating event and develops the following sequences of events that describe potential loss event, accounting for both the successes and failures of the safety functions as the accident progresses. In technical risk assessment they are is used to generate the F/N Curve. This presents a distribution of the size of a loss in terms of fatalities vs. frequency and can be easily adapted to frequency vs. lost revenue

Adapting the system to detailed political risk assessment involves constructing a set of event trees which represents the development of each potential failure or loss case to all the possible event outcomes. The analysis begins with an initiating event and develops the sequences of events that describe potential loss scenarios, accounting for both the successes and failures of the protective functions as the failure or loss event progresses. Event trees are utilised to distinguish between possible outcomes from a single initiating event, based upon a variety of probabilistic parameters such as the probability of sub events and the adequacy or otherwise of protective systems. The general procedure for event tree analysis contains five steps:

- Identifying an initiating event of interest and the correct level of resolution.
- Collecting the relevant probability data and assumptions.
- Identifying protections systems designed to deal with the initiating event.

- Constructing the event tree.
- Describing the resulting sequence of unwanted events.

In this case of an engineering risk assessment a major Liquid Petroleum Gas release and the subsequent ignition or explosion route might be the subject investigated. In the case of political risk some of the following might be the subject of investigation:

- Revolution.
- Coup d'etats.
- Civil war.
- Fractional conflict.
- Ethnic/religious turmoil.
- Widespread riots
- Terrorist attacks
- National strikes, protests, or boycotts
- Shifts in public opinion.
- Union activism.
- Nuclear war.
- Conventional war.
- Border conflicts.
- Alliance shifts.
- Embargoes and international boycotts
- Burdensome external debt servicing requirements
- International economic instability.

Engineering event trees are used to estimate the probability distribution of events leading to fires and explosions with the potential for loss of life. The same rationale may be applied to the stages leading to an event that imposes financial impacts on a project.

SIMULATION

Event tree analysis has the further advantage that it can be the basis of simulations (an increasingly widely used tool) in order to generate probabilistic distributions, as follows:

- Develop event trees that describe each event leading to a final outcome such as a fire, explosion, or unacceptable economic cost.

- Obtain or calculate probability data (either mean value or a distribution) for each leg of the event tree.
- Couple the various outcomes to consequence analysis models which evaluate the potential effects in terms of loss of life, property, interruption to business, or loss of investment
- Run a simulation (using Monte Carlo techniques) over a large time period in order to generate a stable distribution of effects.

ACTIVITY 5: CONSEQUENCE ANALYSIS

Consequence analysis forms an essential part of any risk assessment. At this stage in the analysis the key events identified during Activity 2 and viewed as statistically relevant are assessed using a range of methods in order to quantify the damages arising from the failure events. These effects might include environmental impact, (e.g. oil spills at sea, poisoning of food-producing land), fatalities and property damage (e.g. offshore installations, ships, and industrial installations). In the case of political risk assessment, effects might include the financial impact of events such as ethnic conflict, religious strife, mass protests, riots, terrorism, strikes, boycotts, shifts in public opinion, union activism, civil war, international war, border conflicts, alliance shifts, international boycotts, high external debt payments, and international economic instability.

Just as many of the concepts and procedures of technical risk analysis can be applied to political risk analysis, many of engineering's computer-based algorithms can be applied to political risk analysis. These tools can be used to run experiments and model the effects of key events. Paralleling the development of systematic technical risk analysis, the arbitrary checklists and scoring systems based on subjective assessment can be replaced by deterministic or stochastic models. These models can provide useful information to businesses on how various initial conditions can lead to costly delays, burdensome expenses, and other forms of loss.

ACTIVITY 6: IMPACT ASSESSMENT

The objective of this activity is to assess the potential impact of the various failure cases in terms of agreed damage categories for losses associated with interruptions to budget, specification, time. Inevitably, such an assessment is subjective and has to be based on the experience of the individuals involved in the exercise. Prior to a specific study rule sets are developed with the client on a project by project basis. Categorisation can be as simple as definition of Low, Moderate, Severe, Major or Catastrophic.

The output from this exercise is presented in the form of a set of loss level categories. In the case of a political risk assessment it would cover investments failures and in the case of a technical assessment of lost production and personnel fatalities.

ACTIVITY 7: RISK SUMMATION

Risk has been defined as the product of the consequence of an undesirable event with the likelihood of its occurrence. The objective of this activity is to calculate the impact due to political risk for each failure case identified and then to sum these to give overall risk estimates for the whole investment. The process is subdivided into the following steps:

- Evaluation of all feasible outcomes of a wide range of alternative scenarios.
- Evaluation of the potential impact from the consequence analysis in the form of a probable loss event.

The output from the event trees discussed in Activity 4 is used to determine the frequency of the different possible outcomes of the initial event: this includes probabilities defining the relative likelihood of each possible outcome.

The results of the consequence modelling are combined with each of the corresponding event frequencies and summed to provide overall risk estimates for each aspect of the investment. This then enabled the major risk contributors to be identified and ranked.

ACTIVITY 8: RISK RESULTS

F/N curves are used to present the relationship between the severity and probability of a consequence class. As well as generating overall risk measures for the system being studied, the contributors to each risk measure were ranked to show which dominates. Using F/N curves also enables analysis of all operational, investment and political risk to be presented and compared with other similar commercial schemes.

Figure 3: FN Chart

Frequency Class		Non Prohibitive	Prohibitive	Prohibitive	Prohibitive	Prohibitive
	Likely	Non Prohibitive	Prohibitive	Prohibitive	Prohibitive	Prohibitive
	Occasional	Non Prohibitive	Non Prohibitive	Prohibitive	Prohibitive	Prohibitive
	Unlikely	Non Prohibitive	Non Prohibitive	Non Prohibitive	Prohibitive	Prohibitive
	Rare	Non Prohibitive	Non Prohibitive	Non Prohibitive	Non Prohibitive	Prohibitive
		Non Prohibitive	Non Prohibitive	Non Prohibitive	Non Prohibitive	Prohibitive
	Extremely Rare	Acceptable	Non Prohibitive	Non Prohibitive	Non Prohibitive	Non Prohibitive
		Acceptable	Non Prohibitive	Non Prohibitive	Non Prohibitive	Non Prohibitive
		Negligible	Moderate	Severe	Major	Catastrophic
Consequence Class						

ACTIVITY 9: ASSESSMENT OF RESULTS

The calculated risks are then reviewed so as to assess their significance. The advantage of developing a formalised risk assessment tool in the form of event trees and spreadsheets, is that it facilitates conducting sensitivity analysis of differing assumptions. Such flexibility is extremely important in political risk analysis because of the inevitable high degree of subjectivity in the field.

It is important to recognise that QRA is not an exact science (it is perhaps best characterised as a craft) and that the main advantage of the exercise is not in the generation of absolute numbers but in the ability to compare alternative projects, investments, or geographical sites of operations, and assess the costs of alternative business activities. For example, high risk areas can be highlighted and the causes of the high risks can traced back to their major causes. Any of the assumptions leading to the specification of the cases or their frequencies can be checked and may be refined easily. Ways of reducing significantly their contribution to the risk can be devised and their effectiveness assessed by recalculating the risks.

POLITICAL RISK ASSESSMENT TOOL

Clearly the above represents a complex process especially if there is a requirement to undertake a degree of "What If" analysis which requires numerous modification to the basic input data. Thus DBA and PRS have developed a computerised tool for holistic risk management, called HOLRIM, which enables easy modifications of the basic assumptions and allows comparisons of different investments based on a probabilistic risk assessment.

Figure 4: Schematic of HOLRIM, the DBA-PRS Political Risk Assessment Tool

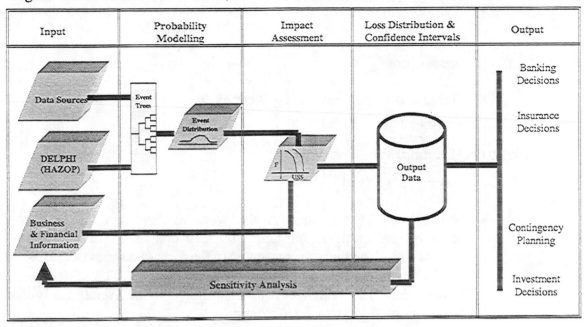

INPUT TO THE DBA POLITICAL RISK ASSESSMENT PROGRAM

The input to HOLRIM consists of:

PROBABILISTIC DISTRIBUTION AND VALUES FOR THE ESTIMATION OF EVENTS

- Revolution, coup d'etats, civil war, fractional conflict, ethnic and religious turmoil, riots, terrorism, strikes, protests, boycotts, shifts in public opinion, union activism, war, border conflicts, alliance shifts, international embargoes and boycotts, high external debt servicing, international economic instability.

DELPHI-GENERATED INFORMATION

- Adverse policy decisions regarding the economy, increased restrictions on investment, altered policies regarding international trade, changes in taxes, and changes in governments.

BUSINESS & FINANCIAL INFORMATION

- Probabilistic cash flow forecasts, accountancy information and details that relate to the budget of the project or investment.

TECHNICAL INFORMATION

- Technical information of engineering, construction, maintenance, and management.

OUTPUT OF HOLRIM

HOLRIM's output consists of:

- Probabilistic distributions in the form of FN Curves which plot consequence in financial terms of interruptions in investment vs. probability. The output is presented in the form of a series of curves for each country being investigated.
- Histograms identifying the major contributors to the overall risk profile of a country or geographical location.

A BRIEF CASE STUDY OF SOME OF HOLRIM'S CAPABILITIES

One key to applying technical methods to political risk analysis is to formulate policies and politics in a host country in terms that allow computer analysis. One set of such formulations is to estimate the probability of each of a series of regimes being in power in a country of interest, and to further estimate the probability that each regime will carryout policies that can adversely affect a business project. Once this has been done, many of the conventionally accepted risk analysis procedures can be applied to political risk analysis.

Consider, for example, the political situation in Venezuela at the beginning of 2000. President Hugo Chávez, a charismatic, populist president, had just secured passage of a radical new constitution that contained many provisions considered threatening to business operations. The constitution decreed minimum protections for workers, guaranteed social welfare benefits, authorised government involvement in the economy, and protected national control of natural resources. If Chávez used his political power to carry through with legislation to impose the most extreme provisions of the constitution, the operational environment for many businesses would sharply deteriorate. Alternatively, the president might choose to move much more slowly and carefully, increasing social welfare and adding some restrictions, but acting much more moderately and slowly so as to allow business to adapt to the new conditions. As a third possibility, new elections might activate the opposition to Chávez, and lead to a return to fractious, divided government that has recently characterised Venezuelan policy-making.

These alternatives can be defined as regimes whose probability can be estimated through a modified Delphi method called the Prince system of political forecasting. (The procedures for calculating regime probabilities from Delphi inputs are incorporated into HORIM.)

To simplify the presentation of the analysis, we will assume that a bank or other financial firm is contemplating the future of its operations in Venezuela. It has estimated the level of costs that it can bear (in terms of taxes, fees, and satisfying regulatory requirements) and still conduct profitable operations in the country. Furthermore, the firm's political risk manager has assigned the level of such costs that are likely to be imposed by the alternative regimes, as summarised in the table below, as of the beginning of 2000:

Regime	Probability	Level of Acceptable Costs to be Imposed
Pragmatic Chávez	55%	44%
Populist Chávez	30%	93%
Divided Government	15%	80%

Several conclusions can be derived from merely inspecting this table. If the regime forecasts hold up and the most likely regime (a Pragmatic Chávez) dominates policy making, then the costs imposed by the government will be only 44% of the maximum acceptable level, a comfortable margin for the firm. On the other hand, the chances of an alternative to a pragmatic regime are not insignificant. And the two alternatives would impose substantially higher costs, in the case of a Populist Chávez the expected costs would be in the danger zone of the firm's profitability.

Some more careful analysis is also possible. Given the probabilities of each of the three most likely regimes, a weighted average can be calculated to estimate the expected level of imposed costs. Such a calculation (provided by HORIM) gives an expected cost level of 64%, substantially higher than the expected cost under a pragmatic Chávez, but still within an acceptable range.

Of course, such a calculation assumes the validity of the estimation of the three regime's probabilities. The Delphi method used to assess such probabilities has been widely used and tested in a variety of political and cultural contexts; nevertheless, it would be foolish to assume that such forecasts are copper bottom guaranteed. In fact, either of the regimes has a potential probability ranging from 0% to 100%. The prudent risk assessor will consider the range of probabilities for each regime being considered. The Monte Carlo methods of HORIM allow for such assessment to be undertaken. First, as the table below indicates, there is a wide range of imposed costs based on the differing probabilities of the three regimes. (We have simplified this illustration by considering only three alternative regimes. In a full Monte Carlo simulation, HORIM could consider a wider range of alternative regimes.)

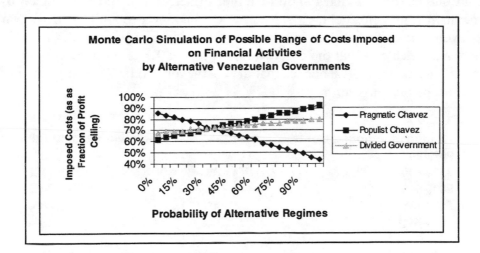

As the figure shows, the range of imposed costs can vary widely around the expected (weighted average) value of 64%. In fact, given the inclinations of the three alternatives and the range of their possible probabilities, the risk profile of Venezuela is substantially more ominous. Consider the next figure, which shows the range of expected imposed costs, taking account of the range of probabilities of all three regimes. As it shows, there is a substantial range of costs approaching the firm's maximum acceptable level.

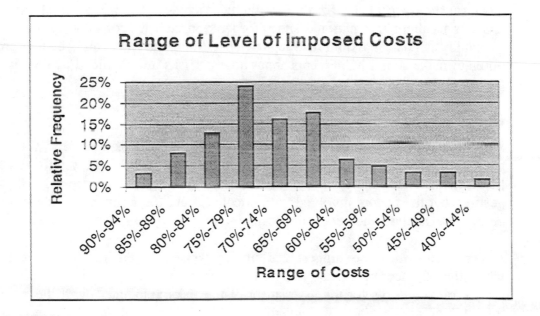

A final output from HORIM shows another dimension of the risks faced by the financial firm in Venezuela. It shows the cumulative probability of the various cost levels, given the probability ranges of the three regimes. As it indicates, there is a 24% chance that the costs will be at least 80% of the maximum the firm can bear, and nearly a 50% chance that the cost level will be 75% or greater of the firm's acceptable maximum.

Range of Imposed Costs	Percentage	Cumulative Percentage
90%-94%	3%	3%
85%-89%	8%	11%
80%-84%	13%	24%
75%-79%	24%	48%
70%-74%	16%	63%
65%-69%	17%	81%
60%-64%	6%	87%
55%-59%	5%	92%
50%-54%	3%	95%
45%-49%	3%	98%
40%-44%	2%	100%
Total	100%	

By considering the range of probabilities (a prudent course in the face of such uncertainties) it is clear that there are substantial risks of the imposed costs being dangerously close to the firm's maximum acceptable level. By applying such analysis to alternative national sites of operation, and by considering alternative risk analysis under possible restructured operations, the firm can use such procedures to make sound judgements about how its risks are balanced against its opportunities.

CONCLUSION

This paper has introduced the application of formal risk assessment as practised by the engineering industry to the political risk arena. Many will view political risk as being more difficult to assess than process or engineering risk, suggesting that the factors involved in political risk are too complex to identify, too complex to analyse and hence, impossible to predict.

To such critics, we suggest that similar concerns were raised in the 1970s when the engineering industry first started to move away from checklists and simple ranking tools for the assessment of the risks associated with the processing, storage and carriage of dangerous materials. The building of a model that may be used to provide help to decision-makers is a lengthy activity. Very often, it is necessary to initiate the model concept long before there is adequate data available. For example, in the early 1970s the engineering industry had carried out very little research which attempted to predict the effects of cryogenic spills of land and water or determine what fraction of the spill would discharge as a liquid and what fraction would discharge as a vapour. Such information became vital if the effects of fires and explosions were to be adequately assessed as defined by the early consequence analysis packages. In the same way, reliability data of key engineering components were inadequately documented prior to the development of more sophisticated reliability and availability modelling techniques. We are currently collecting data and using it as an input to the political risk assessment model. We have currently run this model on a number of projects and are seeking additional projects for testing its parameters.

REFERENCES

1.   R. Rodriguez & E. Carter, International Financial Management, 2nd (Englewood Cliffs, N.J. Prentice Hall 1976 pp385

Chapter 6

📖

Governmental Attributes in Political Risk
Llewellyn D. Howell

Objectives of This Study

This study has multiple objectives that are directed at political risk analysis (theory and model) and political risk assessment (ratings and forecasts). First, I will examine three models and their data to compare [a] the extent to which each model accurately forecasts losses that have socio/political origins, and [b] the extent to which the models are consistent in two time periods (1986 forecasts and 1992 forecasts). Second, I will make a comparison among the models for the two time periods to determine the extent to which forecasts and their source variables change over time. Third, I will focus on the role played by the variables in each model that focus on democracy and democratic institutions. In effect I will be examining the widely held proposition that *the more democracy there is in a country, the better the investment climate for foreign investors will be.* Each of the models contains one or more variables that relate directly to the extent of democracy in the host country for the investor. The first and second objectives are essentially analytical matters; the third is a matter of assessment.

Political risk assessment indices have long been a part of information available to foreign investors who want to prepare themselves for business development in countries where they know little about societal and political underpinnings. Most of the available ratings are provided as a single country rating, not broken down for specific industries, firms, or projects. That is, they are provided at what is referred to as a "macro" level.[1] This is where an action by a government affects all, or nearly all, foreign investors in the country or all investors of a particular type. However, most actual risk is at the "micro" level, directed not only at a particular industry (such as in the expropriation of power plants) but at a specific nationality (e.g. American power plants) or a specific firm.

---

[1] John D. Daniels and Lee H. Radebaugh, *International Business: Environments and Operations, 9th Edition*, Upper Saddle River, NJ: Prentice-Hall, 2001, pp. 99-101.

If the firm wants to learn something about the specific level of political risk in a country for themselves, they must be able to have access to more refined information than just a country level risk rating. They must be able to look at the data for individual variables, the variable weights in the country model, and the structure of the model itself. In creating a firm-specific model, managers may narrow the variables to those that are likely to create conditions that affect their business domain and exclude those variables that do not.[2] In this study I am examining the role of individual variables, first singly and then in combination, in projecting political losses. This will do two things that are useful for a firm's strategic managers: first, it will indicate which variables are particularly effective in projecting losses to foreign investors (and, of course, which are not). Secondly, it will suggest which combinations of variables are most effective in projecting losses. On this basis, variables may be included or discarded when moving from macro to micro levels of assessment.

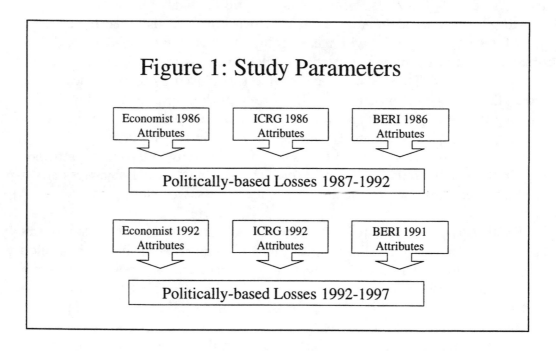

Figure 1: Study Parameters

---

[2] Political Risk Services (PRS) narrows its forecasts to three basic industries: financial transfers, foreign direct investment (FDI), and exports. The IHS Energy Group narrows its model even further to encompass only those variables that have an apparent effect on the petroleum industry, a narrower specialization within FDI. See the PRS and IHS Group chapters (11 and 12) in Llewellyn D. Howell, ed., *The Handbook of Country and Political Risk Analysis, 3rd Edition*, East Syracuse, NY: The PRS Group, 2001.

One variable that has received constant attention since the rise of systematic political risk assessment in the 1960s is the nature of government. While "stability" has received regular attention, its meaning has become less clear over the years as questions have arisen about the interrelationship between stability and type of government. Is the instability of an authoritarian government likely to have the same effects on foreign businesses as the instability of a democratic one? Instead of dealing directly with this potential ambiguity, attention has turned to the type of government that is stable or unstable. Lead questions in risk assessments are now often "Is the country a democracy or a dictatorship? Is power concentrated in the hands of one person or one political party?"[3]

Since the end of the Cold War and the onset of market economies in former and nominally Communist countries, the question of the interrelationship between democracy, transparency, and foreign investor success has grown increasingly common. It became an important element of the Clinton Administration's efforts in China and Vietnam, where it was hoped that successful economic participation would both demand and be more fruitful in more democratic systems. It was likewise argued that systems that were not democratic would founder economically in the market-style systems that became more pervasive as globalization grew during the late 1990s.

The role of democratic institutions remains both philosophically interesting and practically important for foreign investors trying to project their safety and success. In this study, I will explore the wide range of variables that are presented in the three models but will focus on this timely question. Does it make any difference to foreign investors if the government of the country is democratic or not? In answering this question, we will see where this and other variables fall into the ordered scheme of things.

Study Design

Three sets of forecasts from respected companies[4] are compared for two time frames with the objective of determining which models are most successful in

---

[3] Ricky W. Griffin and Michael W. Pustay, *International Business: A Managerial Perspective, 2nd Edition*, Reading, MA: Addison-Wesley, 1998, p. 311.

[4] For a full description of each of these systems as they were applied in the generation of the data used here, see "Countries in Trouble," *The Economist*, December 20, 1986 and William Coplin and Michael O'Leary, eds., *The Handbook of Country and Political Risk Analysis*, East Syracuse, NY: The PRS Group, 1995.

providing useful forecasts. This has the effect of suggesting which of the three theories of political risk assessment is more useful. The models employed are from *The Economist*, Business Environment Risk Intelligence (BERI), and the International Country Risk Guide (ICRG).[5] Each of the models provides an index of risk for countries that is created through assessments of multiple variables that are weighted to reflect importance as a source of risk.

In the first analysis, forecast data from 1986 are correlated with a loss index reflecting politically-sourced losses to business in the years 1987 to 1992[6], the five-year period following the forecast. In the second analysis, late 1991 or early 1992 risk forecasts are compared with a loss index for the years 1992 to 1997. The time periods, with analyses of the three models, are examined in turn with both across model comparisons within the time period and across time period comparisons for each model.

Approaching the comparisons as they are described in "Figure 1: Study Parameters," each of the six separate sub-studies is presented below in this sequence: Model description, 1986 correlations and regression, 1992 correlations and regression. The models are covered in this order: *Economist*, BERI, ICRG. There is some general discussion in each case but the observations and conclusions are presented in the form of propositions (P) with the model source of the proposition labeled with its beginning letter: *Economist* (E), BERI (B), and ICRG (I). From the correlation matrices, the propositions are based on those coefficients that are significant at the .05 level or lower. Regression results are used in ordering variable impact, not as tests of the models themselves.[7]

---

[5] A similar study that compared The Economist, BERI, and the PRS methods for 1986 forecasts only appeared in Llewellyn D. Howell and Brad Chaddick, "Models of Political Risk for Foreign Investment and Trade: An Assessment of Three Approaches," *Columbia Journal of World Business*, Vol. XXIX, No. 3, Fall 1994, pp. 70-91, and in Llewellyn D. Howell, "Social and Political Risk in the New Global Economy: Critical Issues in Forecasting," in Carmen Ghiselli and Frank Hoy, eds., *Challenging Assumptions* (Proceedings of the 1994 Family Firm Institute Conference), Brookline, MA: FFI, 1995, pp. 81-99.

[6] For a description of this Index and the data creation method, see Llewellyn D. Howell, "Operationalizing Political Risk in International Business: The Concept of a Politically-based Loss," in Jerry Rogers, ed., *Global Risk Assessments Book 4*, Riverside, CA: GRA Inc., 1997.

[7] The SPSS program used pair-wise deletion in determining the correlation coefficients and the regression results.

The Economist Model

The Economist model was generated in a study that appeared in the December 20, 1986 issue of the publication. The overall model was a "country risk" model containing political, social, and economic/financial variables with a total rating value of 100 points. The variables that represented "political" risk as defined in terms of outcome losses that could be covered by political risk insurance were ten in number. *The Economist* chose six political variables worth a total of 50 points in weight and four social variables worth 17 points to represent this risk. Each of the variables was given a weight that became the maximum worst score that the country could get. A score of zero meant no risk, the full weight score meant that there was prohibitive risk. The variables that we will focus on here are "**Authoritarianism**," as fairly direct measure of the "democracy" focus here, and "**Generals in Power**," the extent to which the military has influence in political processes and outcomes. They are described briefly below.[8]

The Economist Variables and Weights

Bad Neighbors - 3 negative points: *The Economist* recognized the situational context as being a critical political variable. They argued that being near any super-power almost automatically meant trouble in that superpowers tend to control their peripheries, often with the use of force. Troublespots are those with a history of being "disturbed" or with historically continuous violence. They cite the Middle East and South Africa as examples.

Authoritarianism - 7 points: Whether totalitarian or authoritarian, the lack of democracy in a state forebodes ill: even rigid totalitarian control is only a temporary holding pattern; disruption and probably violence will seethe underneath.

Staleness – 5 points: The argument is that a leader needs about five years to get his or her bearings and a grip on the situation but that after ten years he begins to get detached and stale. Complacency accompanies entrenchment, along with its siblings corruption, disdain, and delay.

---

[8] See Llewellyn D. Howell, "Political Risk and Political Loss for Foreign Investment", *The International Executive*, Vol. 34, No. 6, November-December 1992, pp. 485-498, for a more in-depth discussion.

Illegitimacy – 9 points: Legitimacy implies an uncoerced and positive acceptance on the part of the population of a state. Political risk is a function of the gap between acceptability and a government's persistence in power.

Generals in Power – 6 points: In response to instability or the lack of competent civilian authority (or the military's perception of competent), military authorities often step in and take control themselves. *The Economist* argues that most military men do not know how to govern nor how to step aside gracefully.

War/Armed Insurrection – 20 points: War, the most impactful of any of the variables selected, clearly penetrates the investment picture in a number of ways. Apart from the obvious destruction of physical plant, war disrupts the economy and brings about losses in a number of other ways. Raw goods and supplies are delayed or diverted to war use.

Urbanization Pace – 3 points: When the urbanization process is too rapid, or is too concentrated on a single city, a number of problems accompany the shift. These include 'idleness and crime', an expansion of the drug trade, and economic irregularities, such as in the pricing of food. It is not the fact of urbanization itself but rather the nature of the process and its effect on the society that threatens the foreign investor.

Islamic Fundamentalism – 4 points: *The Economist* argues that there was never much political fervor in Hinduism or Buddhism and that Christianity is a spent force. But, they continue, Muslim radicals could still change the world and where they are strong, the risk to investors is high, especially when the investors are foreign and not Muslim.

Corruption – 6 points: Corruption exists everywhere. U.S. federal department scandals at the end of the Reagan administration and Savings and Loan problems into 1991 reflect its impact in the United States. But in some cases, it has gotten out of hand. Corruption can distort the economy is ways that the best of investor awareness or even power cannot accommodate.

Ethnic Tension – 4 points: Ethnic, religious, and racial tension provide an environment in which simple industry does not suffice. It may redirect government attention, invoke restrictions on investors (hire this group and not that one), restrict labor resources, or result in open conflict. Governments may fall on the basis of its convolutions.

Observations on *The Economist* for 1986 (Tables 1 & 1A)

Proposition *Economist* 1: If the index created by the combined political and social variables (composing political risk) is used to try to forecast actual losses (represented by the index), *The Economist* Index is of little use to the investor. The correlation with the loss index for 1987-92 is only .30 and it is not significant at the .05 level.

Economist 1986	Loss Index	Econ.Pol Risk Index	Super	Auth	Long	Legit	Generals	War	Urban	Islam	Corrupt	Ethnic
Loss Index	1.00											
Economist Cum. PR Index	0.30	1.00										
Superpower/Troublespot	0.28	0.29	1.00									
Authoritarianism	0.10	0.65	0.11	1.00								
Longevity	0.21	0.45	0.21	0.07	1.00							
Legitimacy	0.22	0.68	0.13	0.56	0.34	1.00						
Generals in Power	0.20	0.65	0.06	0.40	0.02	0.49	1.00					
War	0.23	0.81	0.19	0.24	0.00	0.12	0.46	1.00				
Urbanization	-0.31	-0.10	-0.17	-0.08	-0.14	-0.09	-0.09	-0.07	1.00			
Islamic Fundamentalism	0.01	0.46	0.18	0.36	0.23	0.17	0.19	0.24	-0.16	1.00		
Corruption	0.22	0.65	0.00	0.41	0.31	0.26	0.36	0.43	-0.03	0.33	1.00	
Ethnic, Religious, Racial Tensions	0.17	0.63	0.05	0.23	0.16	0.45	0.21	0.58	-0.26	0.23	0.44	1.00
** Significant at 0.01 level												
* Significant at 0.05 level												

TABLE 1: Economist Correlation Matrix 1986

PE2: No individual variable from *The Economist* model has a significant correlation with the Loss Index. The best predictor variable is "Urbanization" at R = -.31 but its direction is reversed from that hypothesized. That is, if the result were reliable it would be telling the investor that the *more rapid* the pace of urbanization, the *less risk* there is to investors!

PE3: Some expected correlations occur among the independent risk variables, helping establish validity to the data generally. Longevity (staleness) correlates highly with authoritarianism (R = .67); Illegitimacy correlates highly with Authoritarianism (R = .56); Ethnic Tensions correlates highly with War & Civil Strife (R = .58); Generals in Power correlates highly with Illegitimacy (R = .49). There are others of note.

PE4: While the result is not significant, it is interesting to note that Islamic Fundamentalism has the lowest correlation with the Loss Index (R = .01).

PE5: Again recognizing that the results are not significant, neither of the democracy indicators—Authoritarianism and Generals in Power—are among the top correlates of Loss. Whether we use the correlations themselves or the significance measure, *we have to conclude that neither the level of democracy nor the presence of democratic institutions has much to do with potential losses, from political or social sources, to foreign investors.*

Table 1A: *Economist* 1986 Variable Importance Ratings			
Variables in Enter Order	**Correlation to Losses**	**Stepwise R^2 Change[1]**	**Enter R^2 Change[1]**
Ethnic, Religious & Racial Tension	0.13	.010	.016
Urbanization	-0.31	.099	.085
Islamic Fundamentalism	0.01	.023	
Generals in Power	0.20		.027
Legitimacy of Regime	0.22	.017	.018
War	0.23	.012	.026
Corruption	0.22	.045	.026
Authoritarian	0.10	.009	.014
Superpower/Troublespot	0.30	.054	.037
Longevity of Regime	0.21	.025	.027

TABLE 2: The Economist Correlation Matrix 1992

Economist 1992	Loss Index	Pol Risk Index	Super	Auth	Long	Legit	Generals	War	Urban	Islam	Corrupt	Ethnic
Loss Index	1.00											
Pol Risk Index	0.58	1.00										
Superpower/Troublespot	0.32	0.38	1.00									
Authoritarianism	0.44	0.75	0.28	1.00								
Longevity	0.19	0.26	-0.07	-0.06	1.00							
Legitimacy	0.33	0.70	0.20	0.48	0.20	1.00						
Generals in Power	0.56	0.83	0.23	0.50	0.30	0.51	1.00					
War	0.38	0.87	0.35	0.63	0.20	0.53	0.69	1.00				
Urbanization	0.62	0.78	0.20	0.55	0.21	0.58	0.66	0.56	1.00			
Islamic Fundamentalism	0.08	0.50	0.20	0.40	-0.05	0.12	0.50	0.50	0.28	1.00		
Corruption	0.51	0.83	0.29	0.62	0.06	0.17	0.71	0.67	0.73	0.60	1.00	
Ethnic, Religious, Racial Tensions	0.11	0.61	0.16	0.41	0.14	0.33	0.37	0.44	0.39	0.57	0.41	1.00

** Significant at 0.01 level
* Significant at 0.05 level

Observations on *The Economist* for 1992 (Tables 2 & 2A)

For the 1992 data in the Economist model, data were derived from a variety of sources, including other political risk data sets, standardized sources such as the *Economist Intelligence Unit*, news sources, and others. In each case the weighting system for the data was scaled to that employed by the *Economist* model. The rescaling will make no difference to the correlations but will to the magnitude of the risk index itself. The latter, however, is not employed here, so the correlation results should parallel those of the 1986 study. In reviewing the propositions suggested below, keep in mind that the Cold War ended in the interim period between the two analyses, dramatically changing the contours of the emerging markets and resulting in many changes in the acceptability of both capitalism and democracy.

PE6: The *Economist* political risk index, in contrast to the 1986 results, correlates highly with the Loss Index for 1992-97. It therefore is considered useful for investors looking for investment and management advice at the macro level.

PE7: Several individual variables, in contract to the 1986 *Economist* results, are also significantly correlated with the Loss Index. These include both of the democracy indicators: Generals in Power correlates at R = .56 (s<.01) and Authoritarianism at R = .44 (s<.05); Urbanization is now correlated with Loss at R = +.62 (s<.01); Corruption also comes into the picture, correlating with the Loss Index at R = .51.

PE8: In a measure of consistency with the 1986 results, some intercorrelations among the independent variables remain high where we would expect them to: Illegitimacy and Authoritarianism correlate at R = .48 (s<.01); Ethnic Tension and War/Civil Strife correlate at R = .44 (s<.01); and more.

PE9: Islamic Fundamentalism, consistent with the 1986 results, is the weakest individual predictor of the Loss Index.

PE10: For our democracy study, we note that Authoritarianism, Generals in Power, and Illegitimacy are highly intercorrelated and are highly correlated with the Loss Index. In this post-Cold War period, the presence of democratic institutions and their parallel conditions does provide an important element in a safe investment atmosphere, at according to the *Economist* model.

Table 2A: *Economist* 1992 Variable Importance Ratings

Variables in Enter Order	Correlation to Losses	Stepwise R^2 Change	Enter R^2 Change
Ethnic, Religious & Racial Tension	0.11	.003	.011
Urbanization	0.62	.379	.390
Islamic Fundamentalism	0.08	.057	
Generals in Power	0.56	.032	.054
Legitimacy of Regime	0.33	.020	.004
War	0.38	.006	.000
Corruption	0.51	.008	.001
Authoritarian	0.44	.017	.021
Superpower/Troublespot	0.32	.043	.040
Longevity of Regime	0.19	.003	.010

The BERI Model

BERI (Business Environment Risk Intelligence) is a corporate entity that provides a complete picture of country risk based on a set of quantitative indices developed and refined over a 25-year period. A comprehensive Profit Opportunity Recommendation (POR) is a macro risk measure and is an average of three ratings, each on a 100-point scale. The Political Risk Index (PRI) is composed of ratings on 10 political and social variables. The Operations Risk Index (ORI) includes weighted ratings on 15 political, economic, financial, and structural variables. The third index is the R Factor (Remittance & Repatriation), also a weighted index, covering the country's legal framework, foreign exchange, hard currency reserves, and foreign debt. The POR thus represents all aspects of country risk. Risk is calculated for the present, as well as one-year and five-year time frames. In this study, I am employing the BERI PRI data, for the "Present" assessments. This makes the data comparable to that from the Economist and ICRG, which also provide assessments that are measures of present conditions.

The BERI Index

BERI's experts grade a country's political risk climate by variable, assigning up to seven points for each of the ten variables, including the symptoms. However, an additional value may be assigned to any of the first eight internal or external variables if the condition reflected by the variable is notably favorable for business operations. The total of these bonus points may range as high as 30, making a maximum of 100 points possible if the risk conditions were absolutely perfect. However, this is never the case. If the bonus points total more or less 20, this reflects low risk. If the bonus score is more or less ten, this is moderate risk. If there are no bonus points, this by itself would be an indication of a high risk circumstance. The total of the variable scores, plus the bonus points, becomes the BERI Index for the circumstance cited.

The BERI Variables (all weighted at 7 points plus the possibility of a bonus)

"Internal Causes"

Under internal causes, there are six variables. 1) **Political Fractionalization** - "Fractionalization of the political spectrum and the power of these factions." This political variable is distinct from any of those in the Economist model. It represents divisions among political perspectives in the society, with numbers of perspectives seen as representing a threat to consistency and regularity in political processes. When strength is added to numbers, the score to be assigned is reduced.

2) **Ethnic Fractionalization** - "Fractionalization by language, ethnic and/or religious groups and the power of these factions." This might be considered a social variable as compared to the first "fractionalization", which represented political or ideological thought. Risk would be increased by a compounding of the divisions, as well as by increased power of the distinct groups. This variable parallels the "Ethnic Tension" variable employed in the Economist model.

3) **Restrictive Measures** - "Restrictive (coercive) measures required to retain power". A political variable that can be equated to the "Authoritarianism/ Totalitarianism" variable in the Economist model, "restrictive measures" and the source of such measures is a common concern among political scientists examining state structures and operations. The existence of authoritarianism or the use of coercive measures reflects the prospect of arbitrary action, abrupt changing of rules, and alienation due to a government's handling of the implementation of decisions. While alienation most directly represents the latter, the business firm might be more concerned by the decision-making structure that would or could choose to make use of such measures.

4) **Mentality** - "Mentality, including xenophobia, nationalism, corruption, nepotism, willingness to compromise." This social variable almost seems like a catch-all. There are some cleavages between subgroups of this set. Xenophobia and nationalism, and perhaps willingness to compromise, do indicate something of "mentality". Xenophobia and nationalism are often related. "Willingness to compromise" would appear to be a different dimension, at least, of mentality, A willingness to compromise might well exist among nationalists, depending on the issue. Corruption and nepotism are related to each other but not to the other subvariables. Corruption might even be an indication of an excessive "willingness to compromise", contravening that factor. That is, a willingness to compromise (presumably low risk) might co-exist with a high level of corruption (high risk). Nevertheless, the expert is asked to give a single score for mentality, blending the five, sometimes contradictory factors.

5) **Social Conditions** - "Social conditions including population density and wealth distribution." This social variable parallels the Economist's "urbanization". A number of social ills cited by the Economist are represented in the broadly defined "social conditions", including crime, unemployment, drug use, illiteracy, and health conditions. BERI's wealth distribution adds another dimension, that of disparity between levels of society, as distinct from conditions that are pervasive.

6) **Radical Left Government** - "Organization and strength of forces for a radical left government." This political variable represents the concerns of the 1970s more than that of the 1990s and might better be an indicator of any radical forces. However, for consistency and comparability the same definition has been maintained over the years. It was still appropriate in the 1986 assessment in any case.

"External Causes"

(7) **Dependence on a Hostile Major Power** - "Dependence on and/or importance to a hostile major power." This variable closely parallels the "Bad Neighbors" variable of the *Economist* model, since both clearly indicate a concern about major power involvement. The BERI variable does not, however, incorporate a similar concern about friendly major powers (who can also cause problems with excessive 'friendliness').

(8) **Negative Regional Forces** - "Negative influences of regional political forces." This is parallel to the other half of the "bad neighbors" variable. 'Negative influences' can easily be translated as 'trouble spot' and represents the same concern as that posed by *The Economist*.

"Symptoms of Political Risk"

(9) **Societal Conflict** - "Societal conflict involving demonstrations, strikes, and street violence." This civil strife variable in encompassed by the *Economist's* "War and Civil Strife" variable. Concern is with the nature of the environment of business operations.

(10) **Instability** - "Instability as perceived by nonconstitutional changes, assassinations, and guerilla wars." The focus here is on the expectation of continued viability of the standing government.

For the BERI data, the variable "use of restrictive (coercive) measures to retain power" is the closest we can come to the *Economist* equivalent—Authoritarianism—as a measure of democracy in the host state. That will be our indicator in pursuing our interest in the role of democratic institutions as a part of the foreign investment climate.

TABLE 3: BERI Correlation Matrix 1986

BERI 1986	Loss Index	Pol Risk Index	Hostile	Reg For	Pol Frac	Eth Frac	Restrict	Ment	Soc Cond	Rad L Gov't	Soc Conflict	Instab
Loss Index	1.00											
Pol Risk Index	-0.59	1.00										
Hostile Major Power	-0.34	0.27	1.00									
Regional Political Forces	-0.44	0.58	0.62	1.00								
Political Fraction.	-0.11	0.45	-0.01	0.18	1.00							
Ethnic Fraction.	-0.03	0.56	0.17	0.18	0.04	1.00						
Restrictive Measures	-0.60	0.81	0.23	0.48	0.11	0.38	1.00					
Mentality	-0.46	0.73	0.04	0.37	0.27	0.29	0.58	1.00				
Social Conditions	-0.45	0.84	-0.05	0.39	0.19	0.37	0.76	0.66	1.00			
Radical Left Gov't	-0.35	0.35	-0.08	-0.03	0.61	-0.14	0.01	0.21	0.24	1.00		
Societal Conflict	-0.34	0.76	-0.07	0.18	0.42	0.33	0.55	0.52	0.71	0.45	1.00	
Instability	-0.37	0.82	0.05	0.34	0.31	0.46	0.70	0.52	0.70	0.30	0.71	1.00
** Significant at 0.01 level												
* Significant at 0.05 level												

Observations on BERI for 1986 (Tables 3 & 3A)

For the BERI data and the Loss Indices, the sign of the correlation will be opposite of what was found in the *Economist* correlations. The Loss Index was created to test the *Economist* results and was therefore set up in the same fashion as the Economist scoring, where zero meant no risk and the high scores meant great risk. The Loss Index is set up in such a way that a zero means no loss and a 10 means total loss. The negative correlations between variables and the Loss Index are thus what we would expect.

PB1: The 1986 PRI from BERI does provide a good indication of probable loss in the following five year period. The correlation of R = -.59 for the BERI PRI far exceeds the R = .30 from the *Economist* for the same Loss Index for 1987-92. This Index does seem to have some utility.

PB2: Seven of the independent variables, by themselves are significant predictors of the Loss Index for the following five year period: significant at the .01 level are Restrictive Measures (our democracy indicator), Mentality, and Social Conditions; at the .05 level, also useful predictors are Negative Regional Forces, Instability, Forces for a Radical Left Government, and Societal Conflict, all in that order.

PB3:   High intercorrelations occur where we would expect them: Instability and Societal Conflict (.71), Social Conditions and Societal Conflict (.71 —the contest over resources in a divided society), Restrictive Measures and Instability (.70 – the use of force doesn't generate stability), Social Conditions and Restrictive Measures (.76 – containing the complaints), and others.

PB4: Ethnic and Political Fractionalization seem to play very small roles in the forecasting of losses to foreign investors (non-significant correlations of -.03 and -.11 respectively).

Table 3A: BERI 1986 Variable Importance Ratings

Variables in Enter Order	Correlation to Losses	Stepwise R^2 Change	Enter R^2 Change
Social Conditions	-0.45	.009	.207
Ethnic Fractionalization	-0.03	.003	.020
Societal Conflict	-0.34		.002
Mentality	-0.46	.014	.047
Restrictive Measures	-0.60	.358	.152
Political Fractionalization	-0.11	.047	.000
Radical Left Government	-0.35	.117	.157
Instability	-0.37	.029	.013
Regional Political Forces	-0.44	.019	.050
Hostile Power	-0.34	.054	

TABLE 4: BERI Correlation Matrix 1992

BERI 1991	Loss Index	BERI Pol Risk Index	Hostile Major Power	Neg. Regional Forces	Political Fractn	Ethnic Fractn	Restrictv Measure	Mentlity	Social Condtns	Forces Rad Left Gov't	Societal Conflict	Instablty
Loss Index	1.00											
BERI Political Risk Index	-0.65	1.00										
Hostile Major Power	0.01	0.32	1.00									
Regional Political Forces	-0.37	0.43	0.60	1.00								
Political Fraction.	-0.11	0.49	0.00	0.05	1.00							
Ethnic Fraction.	-0.08	0.49	0.14	0.11	0.22	1.00						
Restrictive Measures	-0.52	0.76	0.22	0.31	0.23	0.21	1.00					
Mentality	-0.68	0.70	-0.07	0.24	0.22	0.26	0.50	1.00				
Social Conditions	-0.72	0.85	0.15	0.19	0.22	0.25	0.71	0.66	1.00			
Radical Left Gov't	-0.41	0.55	0.09	0.04	0.43	-0.07	0.22	0.38	0.49	1.00		
Societal Conflict	-0.43	0.84	0.07	0.17	0.45	0.48	0.56	0.55	0.75	0.54	1.00	
Instability	-0.46	0.77	0.01	0.22	0.28	0.31	0.67	0.52	0.69	0.44	0.68	1.00

** Significant at 0.01 level
* Significant at 0.05 level

Observations on BERI for 1992 (Tables 4 & 4A)

PB5: Like with the Economist model, the BERI PR Index has improved its predictability for losses in the post-Cold War period, gaining from R = -.59 to R = -.65. With the same Loss Index, the BERI risk index provides a better forecast of risk with .65 over the .59 from *The Economist*.

PB6: The intercorrelations among the BERI independent variables has remained basically the same in the two time periods, indicating some consistency and reliability in the data.

PB7: The role of Hostile Major Powers in predicting losses has diminished from minimal to none (the major powers, except for one, have basically gone away).

PB8: Although the democracy indicator, Restrictive Measures, remains a potent predictor of the Loss Index at R = -.52, it is outweighed by the capabilities of two social variables—Social Conditions (-.72) and Mentality, which includes corruption,

Variables in Enter Order	Correlation to Losses	Stepwise R^2 Change	Enter R^2 Change
Social Conditions	-0.72	.522	.522
Ethnic Fractionalization	-0.08	.009	.012
Societal Conflict	-0.43	.045	.022
Mentality	-0.68	.076	.090
Restrictive Measures	-0.52	.006	.000
Political Fractionalization	-0.11		.000
Radical Left Government	-0.41	.028	.009
Instability	-0.46	.014	.001
Regional Political Forces	-0.37	.039	.043
Hostile Power	0.01	.065	

Table 4A: BERI 1992 Variable Importance Ratings

nepotism, nationalism, and willingness to compromise, at -.68. Democracy remains important but the socioeconomic state and its corollaries in the host state are more telling for the potential investor.

The ICRG Model

Another model of long standing and high reputation is that of the International Country Risk Guide (ICRG). The ICRG model provides a comprehensive country risk assessment with a set of variables that are combined at Political Risk = 100 points, Financial Risk = 50 points, and Economic Risk = 50 points. That sum is divided by two to give a single country risk index on a 100 point scale. In this study I am examining only the Political Risk component.

The ICRG Political Risk Variables

Socioeconomic Conditions (Economic Expectations) – 12 Points: "This is an attempt to measure general public satisfaction, or dissatisfaction, with the government's economic policies. In general terms, the greater the popular dissatis-

POLITICAL RISK COMPONENTS Summary

Sequence	Component	Points (max.)
A	Socioeconomic Conditions	12
B	Economic Planning Failures	12
C	Government Stability	12
D	External Conflict	10
E	Corruption	6
F	Military in Politics	6
G	Religion in Politics	6
H	Law and Order	6
I	Ethnic Tensions	6
J	Political Violence	6
K	Civil War Threat	6
L	Party Development	6
M	Bureaucracy Quality	4
Maximum possible rating		**98**

faction with a government's policies, the greater the chances that the government will be forced to change tack, possibly to the detriment of business, or will fall."[9]

Economic Planning Failures – 12 Points: This is a measure of the government's success in managing the economy under recent and current conditions.

Government Stability – 12 Points: "This is a measure both of the government's ability to carry out its declared program(s), and its ability to stay in office."

External Conflict – 12 Points: "The external conflict measure is an assessment both of the risk to the incumbent government and to inward investment. It ranges from trade restrictions and embargoes, whether imposed by a single country, a group of countries, or the international community as a whole, through geopolitical disputes, armed threats, exchanges of fire on borders, border incursions, foreign-supported insurgency, and full-scale warfare."

---

[9] Directly quoted descriptions are drawn from the ICRG presentation in William Coplin and Michael O'Leary, eds., *The Handbook of Country and Political Risk Analysis*, East Syracuse, NY: The PRS Group, 1995.

Corruption – 6 Points: "This is a measure of corruption within the political system. The most common form of corruption met directly by business is financial corruption in the form of demands for special payments and bribes connected with import and export licenses, exchange controls, tax assessments, police protection, or loans."

Military in Politics – 6 Points: "The military is not elected by anyone. Therefore, its involvement in politics, even at a peripheral level, is a diminution of democratic accountability. However, it also has other significant implications. The military might, for example, become involved in government because of an actual or created internal or external threat. Such a situation would imply the distortion of government policy in order to meet this threat, for example by increasing the defense budget at the expense of other budget allocations."

Religious in Politics – 6 Points: "Religious tensions may stem from the domination of society and/or governance by a single religious group that seeks to replace civil law by religious law and to exclude other religions from the political and/or social process; the desire of a single religious group to dominate governance; the suppression off religious freedom; the desire of a religious group to ex press its own identity, separate from the country as a whole."

Law and Order – 6 Points: "Law and Order are assessed separately, with each sub-component comprising zero to three points. The Law sub-component is an assessment of the strength and impartiality of the legal system, while the Order sub-component is an assessment of popular observance of the law. Thus, a country can enjoy a high rating (3.0) in terms of its judicial system, but a low rating (1.0) if the law is ignored for a political aim, e.g. widespread strikes involving illegal practices."

Ethnic Tensions – 6 Points: "This component measures the degree of tension within a country attributable to racial, nationality, or language divisions. Lower ratings are given to countries where racial and nationality tensions are high because opposing groups are intolerant and unwilling to compromise. Higher ratings are given to countries where tensions are minimal, even though such differences may still exist."

Political Violence – 6 points: "This is an assessment of political violence in the country and its actual or potential impact on governance."

Civil War Threat – 6 Points: "The highest rating is given to those countries where there is no armed opposition to the government and the government does not indulge in arbitrary violence, direct or indirect, against its own people. The lowest rating is given to a country embroiled in an on-going civil war."

Party Development – 6 Points: The level of sophistication and involvement of political parties in providing the potential electorate with access to and a choice of the nation's leadership.

Bureaucracy Quality – 4 Points: "The institutional strength and quality of the bureaucracy is another shock absorber that tends to minimize revisions of policy when governments change. Therefore, high points are given to countries where the bureaucracy has the strength and expertise to govern without drastic changes in policy or interruptions in government services."

For the ICRG model, the best democracy indicators are the variables, "Political Party Development" and "Military in Politics." These two are very close to the variables from *The Economist*, "Authoritarianism" and "Generals in Power," and will allow an interesting comparison.

TABLE 5: ICRG Correlation Matrix 1986

ICRG 1986	Loss Index	ICRG Pol Risk Index	Econ Expect	Econ Plan Fail	Leaders	External Conflict	Corrupt	Military in Pol	Religion in Pol	Law & Order	Race & Nat Tension	Civil Strife	Civ War Risk	Pol Party Devmt	Quality Bur'cy
Loss Index	1.00														
ICRG Pol Risk Index	-0.40	1.00													
Economic Expectations	-0.32	0.80	1.00												
Economic Planning Failures	-0.32	0.74	0.87	1.00											
Political Leadership	-0.22	0.77	0.68	0.67	1.00										
External Conflict Risk	-0.27	0.68	0.43	0.32	0.35	1.00									
Corruption	-0.33	0.76	0.53	0.51	0.65	0.31	1.00								
Military in Politics	-0.23	0.76	0.54	0.54	0.57	0.42	0.61	1.00							
Religion in Politics	-0.23	0.50	0.22	0.17	0.18	0.45	0.31	0.37	1.00						
Law & Order	-0.31	0.86	0.64	0.59	0.62	0.52	0.71	0.66	0.35	1.00					
Racial & Nationality Tensions	-0.26	0.58	0.32	0.23	0.38	0.36	0.44	0.29	0.37	0.48	1.00				
Political Terrorism (Civil Strife)	-0.24	0.76	0.51	0.43	0.51	0.60	0.48	0.51	0.43	0.66	0.54	1.00			
Civil War Risk	-0.26	0.81	0.57	0.53	0.56	0.64	0.60	0.58	0.38	0.66	0.52	0.74	1.00		
Political Party Development	-0.29	0.74	0.49	0.45	0.55	0.47	0.67	0.57	0.35	0.65	0.39	0.45	0.48	1.00	
Quality of Bureaucracy	-0.39	0.81	0.70	0.70	0.64	0.40	0.75	0.67	0.28	0.74	0.37	0.42	0.53	0.69	1.00
** Sig at 0.01 level															
* Sig at 0.05 level															

PI1: In 1986, the ICRG political risk index is better than any single variable in the data set at -.40 and is significant at the .05 level. At this level, the ICRG Index is better than that generated by the *Economist* model for 1986 but considerably less capable than that from the BERI model for that year.

PI2: There is an extremely high set of intercorrelations among the ICRG independent variables. The statistical significance of the these intercorrelations can be accounted for by the larger number of cases in ICRG (up to 140 countries) but the correlation magnitudes indicate that the analysts generating the data are very consistent across variables. I don't know if this is good or bad but it ought to be investigated in future research.

PI3: Our democracy indicators: Political Party Development has a low correlation (-.29) with the Loss Index by itself but it is significant (.05). Military in Politics has a lower correlation (-.23) that is not significant. Democratic institutions don't seem to play a big role in a safe investment environment.

Table 5A: ICRG 1986 Variable Importance Ratings

Variables in Enter Order	Correlation to Losses	Stepwise R^2 Change	Enter R^2 Change
Racial & Nationality Tensions	0.26	.007	.065
Economic Planning Failures	0.32	.007	.071
Economic Expectations	0.32		.001
Civil War Risks	0.26		.000
Military in Politics	0.23	.006	.000
Quality of Bureaucracy	0.39	.151	.036
Corruption	0.33	.006	.002
Law & Order Tradition	0.31	.002	.000
Political Party Development	0.29		.000
Political Terrorism	0.24		
External Conflict Risk	0.27	.007	
Political Leadership	0.22	.007	
Religion in Politics	0.23	.016	

TABLE 6: ICRG Correlation Matrix 1992

ICRG 1992	Loss Index	Pol Risk Index	Econ Expect	Econ Plan Fail	Polit Leaders	External Conflict	Corrupt	Military in Politics	Religion in Politics	Law & Order	Race & Nat Tension	Civil Strife	Civ War Risk	Pol Party Devel	Quality Bur'cy
Loss Index	1.00														
Pol Rsk Index	-0.65	1.00													
Economic Expectations	-0.41	0.76	1.00												
Economic Planning Failures	-0.41	0.74	0.95	1.00											
Political Leadership	-0.36	0.68	0.68	0.68	1.00										
External Conflict Risk	-0.21	0.68	0.44	0.48	0.35	1.00									
Corruption	-0.70	0.72	0.30	0.30	0.23	0.39	1.00								
Military in Politics	-0.63	0.83	0.54	0.52	0.53	0.42	0.65	1.00							
Religion in Politics	-0.20	0.47	0.14	0.15	0.02	0.35	0.50	0.38	1.00						
Law & Order	-0.58	0.86	0.48	0.42	0.52	0.54	0.68	0.75	0.41	1.00					
Racial & Nationality Tensions	-0.31	0.73	0.47	0.48	0.46	0.55	0.48	0.51	0.42	0.59	1.00				
Political Terrorism (Civil Strife)	-0.52	0.77	0.49	0.46	0.49	0.43	0.58	0.60	0.32	0.78	0.57	1.00			
Civil War Risk	-0.61	0.91	0.59	0.59	0.58	0.70	0.68	0.76	0.42	0.82	0.64	0.73	1.00		
Political Party Development	-0.45	0.74	0.43	0.44	0.31	0.52	0.71	0.65	0.37	0.64	0.48	0.47	0.62	1.00	
Quality of Bureaucracy	-0.47	0.73	0.46	0.39	0.37	0.35	0.71	0.67	0.33	0.71	0.40	0.54	0.63	0.65	1.00
** Sig at 0.01 level															
* Sig at 0.05 level															

Observations on ICRG for 1992 (Tables 6 & 6A)

PI4: In 1992, the ICRG political risk index makes a substantial jump from R = -.40 to -.65 in its correlation with the Loss Index. At -.65, it is equal to the predictive capability of the BERI PRI.

PI5: For the democracy variables, Military in Politics has a substantial predictive capability at -.63—almost as good as the Index—and Political Party Development is at R = -.45. While these are useful, several individual variables are better informants on the troubles a foreign investor might face.

PI6: Corruption has the highest individual variable correlation with the Loss Index at R = -.70, followed by Military in Politics. But also high are Civil War Risk (-.61), Law & Order (-.58), and Civil Strife (-.52), all better than the democracy indicator, Political Party Development.

Table 6A: ICRG 1992 Variable Importance Ratings			
Variables in Enter Order	**Correlation to Losses**	**Stepwise R^2 Change**	**Enter R^2 Change**
Racial & Nationality Tensions	0.31	.012	.095
Economic Planning Failures	0.41	.021	.088
Economic Expectations	0.41		.003
Civil War Risks	0.61	.037	.207
Military in Politics	0.63	.053	.062
Quality of Bureaucracy	0.47	.017	.000
Corruption	0.70	.484	.160
Law & Order Tradition	0.58	.005	.003
Political Party Development	0.45	.021	.020
Political Terrorism	0.52		
External Conflict Risk	0.21	.011	
Political Leadership	0.36	.003	
Religion in Politics	0.20	.039	

Some Supported Conclusions

What have we learned from all this, especially in terms of the questions set out above? The regression results below each correlation matrix will generally support the findings as they are brought forth in the correlation matrices.

1. Of the three models as employed in 1986 (see Figure 2), the BERI Political Risk Index provides the best indication of where business losses will occur (r = .59) in the following five years and accounts for 35% of the variance in the loss variable. In social science terms this is reasonably good but provides little in the way of reassurance for foreign investors;

2. Of the three models as employed in 1991-92 (Figure 2), the BERI PRI and ICRG both provide the best indication of losses, with an improved explanation of variance at 42%. This again is good for social science but still not reassuring for foreign investors.

3. All three models, which have not changed over the period of this study, fit the circumstances of the post-Cold War period better than they fit those of the period prior. It seems, in effect, that the world has changed to fit their structures. This is especially true for the Economist and ICRG models.

4. In none of the models, for either time period, do the external variables (super-power influence or international strife) play a significant role in shaping the investment environment.

5. The increased influence of domestic turmoil and deprivation variables in predicting loss across the two time frames closely parallels the claims payment experience of OPIC, where the paid claims in the 1987-92 period were primarily for Inconvertibility while paid claims in the 1992-97 period were dominantly for Civil Strife Damage (OPIC, 2000);

6. For all of the models, the individual variables that provide the strongest explanatory contribution to variance in future losses (risk) have changed between the two periods. This means that an index with a set of variables and assigned weights created in one timeframe may not be applicable in another timeframe. As the sources of loss change (e.g. the shift from Inconvertibility in the late '80s to Civil Strife Damage in the early '90s), so must the choices of variables that are used to forecast those losses;

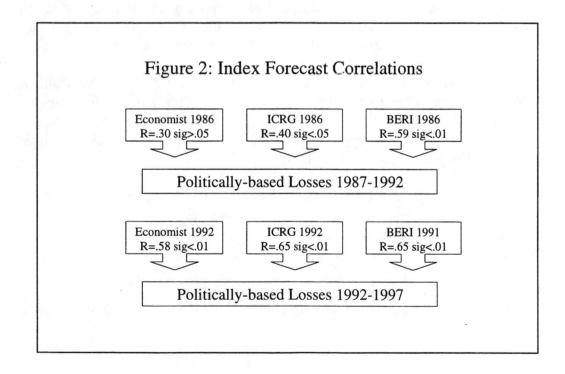

Figure 2: Index Forecast Correlations

Economist 1986	ICRG 1986	BERI 1986
R=.30 sig>.05	R=.40 sig<.05	R=.59 sig<.01

Politically-based Losses 1987-1992

Economist 1992	ICRG 1992	BERI 1991
R=.58 sig<.01	R=.65 sig<.01	R=.65 sig<.01

Politically-based Losses 1992-1997

5. Risk indices created in the 1980s (or earlier) indicate some utility in 1986 but have a vastly reduced predictive quality in 1992, strongly suggesting a need for restructuring. [Noting that ICRG has recently (1998) made some reasonably significant changes in its choice of variable and their weights.]

6. Future losses to foreign investors can be forecast but users need to be familiar with the qualities of indices and be prepared to modify projections to fit particular circumstances.

7. On the question of the role of democracy in making for safe investment environments, from the BERI model with 1986 data we can see that "Restrictive measures" used by the government provides the best explanation of losses in 1987-92. But neither the Economist nor the ICRG models, in 1986, give any support to this role.

8. In the 1992 period, each of the three models indicates a stronger role of democratic institutions in shaping the investment environment than they did in the 1986 period. But it is important to add that in each of the models, other variables surpass the democracy in importance. For the Economist model it is the Pace of Urbanization; for the BERI model it is both Social Conditions and Mentality; for ICRG it is Corruption and Civil War Risk. These results are supported in the regression results that sort out the intercorrelations among the independent variables.

This examination of political risk models is obviously preliminary. But there is sufficient evidence here to argue there is importance in understanding the theories that underlie models such as those utilized here. The varying theories projected through these three models bring varying results and advice for investors. But all three agree in one area of advice: a focus on democratic institutions as a singularly reliable variable in assessing investment environments would be a mistake.

Those who necessarily act for the firm in assessing political risk in foreign ventures must be familiar with both the underlying structure of a forecast and the means of manipulating provided data in ways that better serve the firm's particular interests. And here we have addressed only country-level risk. We have not addressed the questions of industry, firm, or project risk, all of which are selected and unique subsets of country risk. However, we also know that with data provided by the sources examined can result in useful and reliable projections of country risk, and therefore probably also of subset risk. All investing firms need is an understanding that reliable models are necessary for this critical function in foreign direct investment and the will to assign appropriate personnel to adapt existing methods and data.

Chapter 7

Managing Country Risk
in Large Financial Institutions
Roger E. Shields

Country risk is only one of several types of financial risk with which international institutions, both public and private, must deal. Among other types of risk which must be analyzed carefully are credit risk, market risk and operational risk. These latter types of financial risk are better understood even within financial institutions and certainly by non-financial institution participants, than is country risk. When credit is extended it is well understood by creditor and obligor that the obligor may turn out to be a poor credit risk. Anyone who has invested in equities or bonds understands that the value of the equity may rise or fall depending on the direction of market forces. And we understand that a misplaced decimal on a credit card statement due to someone's oversight in the operations division can cause serious problems for the lender or borrower.

Country risk events, on the other hand, are encountered less frequently. Nevertheless, country risk has been a leading cause of the severe problems experienced in many emerging market countries in the last several decades. Country risk was prominent in the Latin America crises of the 1980s. It was also a major factor in the near financial meltdown that occurred in Mexico in 1994-95 and in the problems experienced in 1997-98 in the Asian financial crisis. It has been a problem for Russia and its creditors and most recently has threatened the economic stability of Brazil. While country risk is most obvious when something goes wrong and a country and its creditors face financial and economic trauma, it is also an omnipresent factor in many countries that never figure in crisis situations. These countries are ineligible to borrow in the first place because country risk considerations have made them uncreditworthy. It is clearly a type of risk that large financial institutions operating in global markets have to study and analyze carefully.

Cross-Border Exposure

A large international financial institution will be defined here loosely as one with cross-border exposure of at least several billion dollars spread across many different countries and products. Cross-border exposure arises when credit is extended in a currency other than the local currency of the borrower, or when the funding for the exposure is from offshore sources. A financial institution's exposure may be in local currency but still be classified as cross-border if the exposure was funded offshore. Thus defined, a financial institution's exposure in a foreign country will be classified as cross-border unless it is in local currency and has been funded through local liabilities.

Country Risk

The purpose of this rather formal definition is to identify exposures that are subject to country risk, as opposed to other types of financial risk. While there is no universally acknowledged definition, a useful and generally recognized definition describes *country risk as the risk of default or interruption of debt service or cross border obligations due to an inability or unwillingness of a country to utilize or acquire foreign exchange.* The emphasis here is on the ability of the country as a whole to acquire or make available the foreign exchange needed to service the external debt not just of the sovereign but also of the country's non-sovereign obligors.

The emphasis on the macro environment or level, as opposed to the micro or individual obligor level is important. Credit risk is concerned with the creditworthiness of the individual borrowing entity. *The credit standing of the individual borrower may be impeccable, but the exposure may nonetheless become non-performing because of deteriorating country risk.*

A country can obtain the foreign exchange needed to service its external obligations in a number of ways. Foreign exchange can be earned through export sales of goods and services. A country may also receive foreign exchange in the form of remittances from its citizens employed abroad or from foreigners making direct or portfolio investments in the country. These are all non-debt-producing sources of foreign exchange, although foreign investments will ultimately give rise to a flow of foreign exchange earnings back to foreigners (assuming the investments are productive). Foreign exchange may also be borrowed, with a subsequent need to service the debt as it pays interest and is amortized. Debt service, though, is only one of many uses of foreign exchange. Imports of goods and services and income payments to foreign investors are others.

Country risk concerns arise when aggregate <u>demand</u> for foreign exchange, which also includes capital flight, becomes large relative to its supply. One course of action when that happens is to simply let markets work and allocate foreign exchange as market forces dictate. But that means that capital may be allowed to flee the country. Or, luxury goods may be imported while imports of goods and services deemed vital to the country's interests by governing authorities go unmet.

In that case, the government may decide that scarce foreign exchange must be rationed out to the uses it considers highest and best, and that may not include servicing the debt of those entities that earned the foreign exchange. Capital controls barring the transfer abroad of foreign exchange may be imposed, as Malaysia did for certain classes of capital during the recent Asian financial crisis. Exporters and others who earn foreign exchange may be required to sell foreign exchange to the Central Bank, which will then allocate the foreign exchange to uses set by government priorities. In this situation creditworthy entities with foreign exchange earnings more than sufficient to service their own external debt may find themselves unable to do so. Sound credit risk analysis thus may be deficient in protecting credit exposure because of country risk problems. When serious country risk problems arise, a generalized moratorium declared by a country on the servicing of external debt, or a demand for the restructuring of external debt, may ensnare good credit risks as well as poor ones. These events are hallmarks of country risk crises.

Inseparability of Different Types of Risk

It is useful conceptually to separate the different types of risk, but in practice the distinction is blurred. Financial institutions experience credit losses in even the most solid of countries. Country risk crises will always be accompanied by severe credit risk problems, but he reverse is not true. The weakness of banking systems in Korea, Indonesia, Malaysia and Thailand was underscored in the recent crisis in Asia. The same is true for the 1994-95 Mexican crisis. But Japan, Norway and Sweden, countries with much different country risk profiles, have also had banking system problems which created, and in the case of Japan are still creating, economic and financial problems. Even the United States, with its impeccable country risk rating, suffered a thrift crisis that entailed huge financial costs for investors and taxpayers alike.

Similarly, slow growth and recession have resulted in credit losses in the U.K., the U.S., Germany, France and Japan, the countries with the best country risk ratings in the world, as the business cycle has run its course. Sharp fluctuations in exchange rates have also produced winners and losers in these countries.

Sound country risk fundamentals and accurate country risk analysis are not substitutes for good credit and market risk analysis. Neither Mexico in 1994-95 nor Thailand in 1997-98 resorted to capital controls or a moratorium on debt service, or requested the restructuring of their external debt. Financial institutions with cross-border exposure in those countries have had some obligors that prospered and improved their credit standings before stability returned, while other credits have been written off, victims of exchange-rate movements and recession.

It could thus be argued, although I believe incorrectly, that the major concern in both Mexico and Thailand during their crises was credit, not country risk. It is not clear that either Mexico or Thailand would have been able to avoid such measures as capital controls and debt restructuring in the absence of massive emergency financial support from official lending institutions like the IMF and World Bank as well as bilateral support from other countries. In the case of Korea, short-term debt was restructured even though the crisis was of short duration. In Indonesia the process of restructuring is continuing. In both of these countries, country risk events were clearly part of the crises.

In any case, in Mexico, Korea, Malaysia and Thailand the issue today is credit risk, not country risk. It is clear nevertheless that the two types of risk were mutually reinforcing in a negative direction during the periods of crisis in those countries, and that credit risk today has been magnified by country risk considerations. But changes in the country and credit risk environments do not always go in the same direction. Ironically, *some of the measures needed to improve country risk and place it on sound footing, such as the deliberately induced slow growth and even recession that reduces or eliminates a current account deficit, will worsen the credit risk environment.* It is well understood that the medicine that ultimately cures may cause other interim health problems. In a similar vein, *the sustained rapid growth which may be taken as a sign of successful economic policy may result over time in unsustainable current account deficits that lead to severe country risk problems.* Korea and Thailand are two recent examples of this phenomenon.

Given this interaction between country risk and credit risk, the definition of country risk should be extended to take note of local credit risk related to the economic and political environment, especially in the case of countries with poorer country risk ratings. The country risk analyst will not do extensive forecasts of the advanced economies, except to ascertain the global economic environment that affects countries where country risk is a concern.

Forecasting Country Risk Events

Unlike the credit and market risk analysts, the country risk analyst will find that quantitative models are of limited use in providing predictive power concerning country risk events that lead to financial losses for cross-border creditors. Quantitative models can be built that will predict 100 percent of countrywide credit defaults but they will also predict many times that number that never occur.

Some country risk events are purely political in nature and inherently unforecastable. Iran under the Shah was a staunch ally of the United States. Iranian country risk analysts at that time could reasonably have believed that the largest and most developed economy in the world, their political ally, posed little in the way of country risk for Iranian financial institutions. But the Shah was deposed and went into exile, Iranian militants seized the U.S. embassy in Teheran and Iranian assets in the U.S. were frozen. Similarly, Iraq's invasion of Kuwait took even western government intelligence organizations by surprise.

Some would argue that the situation is not much better with regard to the ability to forecast debt service problems caused by economic factors, and would point to the 1997-98 events in Asia as proof of that assertion. The economic pain and suffering inflicted on the citizens of Hong Kong, Indonesia, Korea, Malaysia and Thailand by those events should not be minimized. But despite the hysteria that described those shocks in 1997 and the follow-on disturbances that occurred in Russia and Brazil in the summer of 1998 as a global financial crisis, reality was substantially different. Aggregate economic growth in the G-7 countries equaled 3.0% in 1997, the same as in 1996 and, with 1996, was the most rapid growth since 1989.

It would be expected that a global financial crisis, such as the réal crisis that occurred in the early 1980s, would have widespread negative country risk impacts, as that crisis did. But the country risk impact of the Asia crisis of 1997-

98 was confined primarily to Indonesia, Korea, Malaysia and Thailand. Hong Kong suffered deep recession, but did not lose its high investment grade rating from the rating agencies. After experiencing a few shock waves, the Philippines separated itself from the crisis countries and continues to record solid economic gains. And in Latin America, Chile, the country most directly affected by the Asian turmoil, developed recession but no external debt problems.

G-7 growth in 1998 equaled 2.2%, with France registering its highest growth rate since 1989, and Germany its highest growth rate since 1991. The U.S. economy surged in both 1997 and 1998 at a rate of 3.9%, the second highest rates in more than two decades. Japan, struggling with its own structural problems since the bursting of its bubble economy a decade ago, did feel the backlash of the problems in Asia's developing economies, which are important trading partners of Japan. Clearly, though, the "global financial crisis" of 1997-98 did not derail world growth in those years.

That should not be surprising. The combined GDP of Hong Kong, Indonesia, Korea and Malaysia equaled less than 4% of world GDP in 1997, while the combined GDP of Russia and Brazil in 1998 was only a little larger in relative terms at about 4.5% of world GDP.

But there is another factor at work here, and that is the nature of the afflicted countries themselves. The strong economic (including external debt) fundamentals of Mexico in 1998, three years after its crisis year in 1995, are far different from the economic profile and structure of Mexico in 1985-6, three years after Mexico became the first explicit manifestation of the Latin American debt crisis in 1982 (and which lingered on through the rest of the decade). Even more striking are the differences between the country risk profiles of Korea, Malaysia and Thailand, all of which had relatively light external debt service burdens as they entered their crisis periods in 1997-98, and the heavily indebted countries of Latin America in the 1980s.

The external creditors of these countries, of both private and public sector borrowers, have certainly incurred credit losses as a result of the Asian crisis, and will experience more losses in the future as these countries correct structural problems. But there has been no general restructuring of external debt or debt service moratorium in Malaysia or Thailand, and no major pain has been experienced by creditors because of the restructuring of short-term debt in Korea. Unfortunately, the same is not true with regard to Indonesia, where the relative external debt service burden was far heavier as the crisis began. Nevertheless, the losses to the external creditors of these countries in 1997-98 were nothing like the losses incurred in Latin America in the 1980s.

Emphasis on External Debt and Liquidity

It is difficult if not impossible to predict the timing or even the probability of country risk events, especially in an era when markets are closely linked on a global basis and the term contagion has taken on new meaning. It is possible nevertheless to say something about what effect these events will have on a country's ability to service its external debts, and to manage cross-border exposure in the presence of these hazards.

A country's economic fundamentals and basic structure are obviously important to its international competitiveness and to its long-term economic progress. They are also important determinants of country risk ratings. Country risk analysis, though, must be more finely tuned. Structural weaknesses were present in Indonesia, Korea, Malaysia and Thailand years before the crises of 1997-98 enveloped these countries. Mexico is not a candidate today for near or even medium-term country risk problems, although its crisis in 1994-95 exposed serious weaknesses in its banking system structure which, while they are being addressed, have not yet been corrected. No one would argue today that Japan's banking system has not suffered from serious structural problems over an extended period. Yet very few would argue that country risk in Japan is not negligible. In the same vein, protracted low growth rates and double digit unemployment rates have highlighted serious structural weaknesses in the economies of France and Germany. Those weaknesses, however, have not impaired their country risk ratings.

Country risk analysis instead should focus on a country's external debt and liquidity characteristics and on the variables that affect them most immediately and closely, such as the country's balance of payments position, existing balance of payments adjustment mechanisms and the economic policies that influence them.

Overvalued currencies, persistent large current account deficits, rapid buildups in short-term debt, relatively large external debt positions and concerns about reserve adequacy were common themes in the Latin American problems of the 1980s, the Mexican crisis of 1994-95 and the 1998-99 problems in Russia and Brazil. It is these factors and their interrelationships that reveal much about a country's ability to service its external debt.

Country Risk Fundamentals

It is hardly necessary to say that the quality of country risk analysis is dependent not only on the skill, professionalism and experience of the analyst but also on the quantity, quality and timeliness of the country data. Much has been done in recent times to improve the timeliness, quality and scope of coverage of relevant country data, but gaps still exist. Organizations such as the International Monetary Fund (IMF) and the Bank for International Settlements (BIS) have been at the forefront of this effort to improve data collection. The course of the Asian crisis might have been shorter and less severe had Thailand's uncovered forward positions in foreign exchange markets and thus its net reserve position been transparent to market participants in the months leading up to the devaluation of the baht at midyear 1997.

Following are some of the key quantitative indicators that should be considered in developing country risk profiles:

➢ *Ratio of External Debt to GDP* -- This indicator is commonly used to indicate the relative burden of debt service, but in some cases it has limited relevance. Debt service payments must be made from the foreign exchange available to a country; external debt may be low relative to GDP but foreign exchange earnings may also be low, indicating constrained debt service capacity (Brazil is an example). This ratio is also subject to radical deterioration when currency devaluation lowers a country's GDP almost overnight. There are more meaningful debt service burden indicators available.

➢ *Ratio of Interest Service to Foreign Exchange Earnings* – If a country is considered a reasonable risk, the principal component of debt service will generally be rolled over, leaving the interest to be serviced out of export earnings. If interest service requires more than 15% of export earnings, it is an indication that debt service is becoming relatively burdensome.

➢ *Ratio of Debt Service to Foreign Exchange Earnings* – This indicator is commonly known as the debt service ratio. Debt service here includes both interest and amortization of medium and long-term external debt. The assumption, not always a valid one, is that short-term debt will be rolled over. Nevertheless, the debt service ratio is perhaps the single best indicator of the relative burden of debt service. As the *Graph 1* shows, it may offer little clue as to the timing of country risk crises, but it will provide an idea of how severe the systemic problems will be. A consistent value of this ratio over 40% is a danger signal to the country's external creditors.

Malaysia, Korea and Thailand had relatively light debt service burdens when their problems began in 1997. That is, they needed a relatively low portion of their foreign exchange earnings to service external debt. As events proved, the crises for these countries were not debt crises, but liquidity and foreign exchange crises. In contrast, the debt service ratio for Argentina in 1982, when the Latin American debt problems led to widespread defaults, was over 100%, while Brazil's equaled almost 90% and that of Mexico and Chile were just under 70%.

This indicator is straightforward. If a country has to choose between servicing its external debt and sacrificing vital imports over an extended period, the choice will often be in favor of imports.

➤ *Current Account as a Percent of GDP* – A current account deficit must be financed. A current account deficit chronically in excess of 6% is an indication of a basic balance of payments disequilibrium that requires external borrowing to bridge the gap. This debt will have to be serviced, adding to the deficit. In this way the balance of payment problem ultimately becomes an external debt problem. An exception to this general rule may exist when a country is a recipient of substantial direct foreign investment over an extended period. The investment may be the driving force behind the current account deficit.

In addition to quantitative indicators of the relative burden of external debt, there are quantitative indicators of liquidity that can be used to gauge a country's ability to withstand a liquidity crunch. Among these are:

➤ *Official Reserves as a Percentage of Annual Debt Service* – Obviously, the higher the reserve coverage of debt service, the greater the cushion against foreign exchange earnings shortfalls or capital outflows. A 300% value for this ratio is comfortable, while anything below 100% will trigger an alarm. *Graphs 2 and 3* show the vulnerability of the Asian crisis countries in 1997 to the liquidity problems that engulfed them.

Official Reserve Coverage of Total External Debt – A value below 25% is cause for concern. Coverage of 40% or more should be considered ample. The greater the share of short-term debt in total debt, the greater is the need for liquid reserves.

> *Reserve Coverage of Imports* – An old rule of thumb for reserve adequacy stresses the role of reserves as a cushion providing for the continuing flow of needed imports in the event of a bubble temporarily restricting the availability of foreign exchange. Reserves equal to four months of imports were considered adequate in the past. Today, when capital flows across national borders at the flick of a finger on the keyboard, this proposition has less validity.

Although the above listed indicators of country risk can be quantified, it should be emphasized that the interpretation of their meaning and relevance to country risk issues cannot be quantified. Problems with the accuracy and timeliness of data can at times render these indicators almost useless. Even when they are accurate, market confidence or lack of confidence, based on real or unsubstantiated factors, can for even extended periods produce results that seemingly contradict the quantitative indicators.

Economic Policy

That is why it is essential to examine quantitative country risk indicators in the context of economic policy. If economic policy decision-making is sound, the shocks to which all economies are subjected at one time or another and the excesses that develop over the course of the business cycle will either be corrected before a major country risk incident occurs or, if one does occur, the damage will be contained and the economy will be restored to basic health without the country's external creditors incurring major losses.

The quality and consistency of economic policy in its entirety should be considered, but balance of payments adjustment policies deserve special emphasis. Consider the case of Brazil.

Despite rampant inflation in the first half of the 1990s, a flexible and competitive exchange rate prevented serious erosion in the balance of payments even in the presence of rapid growth. The evils of inflation, though, especially at the rates they were occurring in Brazil, could not be tolerated, and Brazil took measures to eradicate its inflation problem. Brazil's assault on inflation worked, as the following table shows.

Brazil

	1992	1993	1994	1995	1996	1997	1998
GDP (%)	-0.5	4.9	5.9	4.2	2.8	3.0	0.3
CPI (%)	986.0	1973.4	2363.6	73.8	15.5	6.0	3.2
Current Account ($ bil.)	6.1	0.0	-1.2	-18.1	-23.6	-33.8	-35.2
Real Effective Exchange Rate (1990=100)	72.5	74.1	85.1	101.1	106.8	109.1	105.3

The cure, however, depended to a great extent on the powerful inflation-damping effects of currency overvaluation. Inflation dropped sharply, but the current account deteriorated. At the same time, Brazil failed to make inroads with regard to its structural fiscal problem. International financial markets were willing to live with rampant inflation so long as the external accounts remained sound, but balked as Brazil's external accounts deteriorated rapidly. The crises that occurred in the summer of 1998 and early in 1999 were the result.

Management of External Debt

The importance of the quality of external debt management can hardly be overstressed. Over-reliance on short-term debt exposes a country to contagion effects from problems in other countries even if its own position is fundamentally sound. The rapid accumulation of short-term debt may also signal the inability of the borrowing country to tap long-term capital, a sure indicator of potential problems.

On the other hand, good management of external debt will match maturities with appropriate uses. Using long-term debt to finance short-term trade may lower a country's vulnerability to sudden termination of short-term credit lines by nervous creditors. But long-term debt has to be amortized, and the amortization of debt that has long been disconnected from the purposes for which it was contracted is also a source of potentially serious problems.

The financing of trade is generally a valid use of short-term debt. It is useful to compare the volume of outstanding short-term debt with imports. Because short-term debt should include long-term debt due within one year, the appropriate relationship between a particular country's trade and its short-term external debt is not always easy to ascertain. In general, short-term debt in excess of six months imports of goods and services should be a signal for closer examination of a country's use of short-term debt.

Banking System and Country Risk

It is also worth paying special attention to a country's banking system. Weak banking systems have figured prominently in all of the major emerging market crashes that have occurred over the past several years. While none of the cataclysmic disturbances can point to weak banking systems as a primary cause, they have been a major factor in determining the shape and speed of economic recovery. Weak banking systems affect country risk in several ways. Several of the most important are noted below.

Weak banking systems may be negatively impacted so heavily that they are unable to finance the exports of even financially sound and competitive companies. This constrains the foreign exchange earnings of a country when needed most.

The generally accepted policy to be followed in the aftermath of a forced currency devaluation and capital outflow is to raise interest rates and tighten fiscal policy in order to prevent currency free-fall and limit inflation stemming from the devaluation. All of the recent episodes of sharp currency pressures and external debt servicing impairments have had an aftermath of high domestic interest rates accompanied by deep recession (Mexico, Thailand, Malaysia, Indonesia, Korea, Russia and Brazil). This combination of high interest rates and steep declines in GDP has weakened banking systems that in most cases were already weak. As banking systems have come under pressure, accumulating loan losses and deteriorating asset quality have caused banks to further restrict liquidity in the economy at a time when greater liquidity is badly needed.

The cost of restructuring and recapitalizing banks may result in pressure on budgets and result in erosion of fiscal balances, contributing to a loss of confidence in the economy and stimulating higher interest rates and inflation. In the case of Thailand, estimates place the annual budgetary cost of bank recapitalization at 32% of GDP.

When domestic credit expansion is consistently high and imbalances in an economy become readily apparent, as, for example, in the real estate sector, confidence in the economy may weaken and capital outflows occur, leading to currency pressure and devaluation. This leads to the vicious cycle of rising interest rates, recession and further weakening of the banking sector. The result is a deteriorating country risk environment.

The Political Environment

An examination of political traditions, institutions and trends is another critical element of country risk analysis. The stability of institutions, traditions which affect issues such as the independence of the central bank and the responsiveness of governments to their citizens all affect economic policymaking. Beyond local political issues, an evaluation of regional political stability is critical for obvious reasons.

Political trends are particularly important as they affect the volatility of economic policy or the ability of a country to change the direction of economic policy when fundamental restructuring is required. Mexico's past cycle of financial crises each presidential election year is famous. Mexican officials claim that the cycle has ended but only careful analysis can suggest whether that cycle will be broken in 2000.

Expropriation, acts of war and interference by the government with contractual arrangements are other country risk hazards that can arise from political acts. Problems with the quality of the legal system usually reflect political issues, and can present significant elements of country risk. Problems with the legal and regulatory systems, however, do not usually present problems of volatility and difficulties in forecasting. They are known entities that in general evolve only slowly over time.

Political risk analysis is fraught with difficulty. To do it as it should be done requires devoting resources to establish a close association with the country being analyzed—close enough to see beyond its formal organization charts. There are many secondary sources that can provide profession political risk analyses, and these sources should be utilized as needed. They are not, however, substitutes for in-house expertise for institutions with large cross-border exposure.

Rating the Countries

Once the economic and political analyses have been completed, countries should be arranged in terms of the degree of country risk they represent. These ratings will form the basis for making the key decisions about the type and relative size of exposures that will be considered for each country.

There are a number of rating systems that have been used successfully. Some use elaborate numerical ratings, based on the relative position of each country with regard to the chosen and weighted country risk indicators. One of the virtues of this approach is the thorough and systematic process which, if done properly, it provides. Nevertheless, the individual numerical rankings assigned to each country cannot mask the fact that the process is still subjective.

Another approach is to establish a small number of risk categories based on the individual needs and preferences of the financial institutions and after a careful and comprehensive review place each country into the category in which it fits best. The result is a classification system that places countries in a risk grade that they share with other countries deemed to have approximately the same amount of country risk.

Typically, the best several categories will be for countries where country risk is deemed to be very small, while the lowest rated categories, usually two or three, will be for countries considered uncreditworthy. The middle grades will be occupied by countries where, although the countries are generally creditworthy, country risk is a factor that will be important in determining the amount, type and tenor of exposure that it will be permissible to undertake.

Since country limits will be heavily influenced by country risk ratings, split ratings have in some instances been assigned to countries, with the second and higher rating restricted to specific classes of exposures. This is based on the premise that countries will place a higher priority on servicing some types of debt than on others. It has been demonstrated, for example, that trade credits have frequently been exempted from debt restructurings. If a country has a history of protecting its trade lines, a split grade may be useful. It could perform the two-fold useful function of allowing larger exposures on a prudent basis and directing exposures toward preferred credit classes.

Whatever the rating system chosen, it should be a process that is under constant review. Countries should be downgraded and upgraded as frequently as changes in a country's circumstances require. Some of the categories, in fact, will be occupied primarily by countries migrating from one category to another several steps away. These are countries in obvious disequalibrium, where policy measures will lead to substantial improvement or deterioration in country risk. At the same time, country grades, to have any real meaning, should have a long-term outlook. Core determinants of country risk will not change with every economic wind that blows.

Setting Limits or Guidelines

Once the quality of country risk has been determined by the country risk study, prudential exposure limits are set. Limits are designed to limit losses in the event of a countrywide debt restructuring, debt service moratorium, expropriation or some other country-risk-driven impairment of debt service. The limit is self-explanatory; it constrains exposure in a country. Limits may set rigid caps on exposure, but in practice they have some flexibility. If risk policy allows for a reasonable amount of flexibility with regard to limits, the term guideline is used in place of limits.

Limits or guidelines should ideally have components relating to the major exposure categories contemplated in each country. Different types of exposures are subject to different aspects of country risk. Trade exposures, as has already been noted, have in some countries been virtually immune to interruptions of debt service when almost all other external debt has been subjected to restructuring. If a creditor's analysis indicates that the borrowing country views trade credit as a preferred, protected class, then limits can be set at correspondingly higher levels for trade exposures. In some countries trade credit may be the only type of exposure undertaken because of a belief that the risks associated with other types of lending are excessive.

The number and description of the limit categories will also depend on the nature of the lender. Local business offices provide opportunities for different types of business than can be done from offshore offices. A competitive advantage in one or several areas may allow the prudent taking on of certain types and amounts of exposure that would otherwise be foreclosed. Limit categories will be created for types of credit extended, and will thus vary from institution to institution.

Limit categories may be restricted to exposures where market risk is not a major issue. Trading limits on a country basis may be set by those primarily responsible for managing market risk.

It is particularly important to differentiate between exposure tenors in setting limits. Short-term (under one year) exposures generally carry less risk than term exposures. One obvious advantage of short-term exposures is the ability they give to reduce exposure reasonably quickly with little or no loss. It is also true that greater confidence attaches to short-term forecasts of economic and financial conditions than to long-term forecasts.

It would be wrong, though, to believe that short-term exposures carry little risk. Many countries have restructured trade credit as well as other short-term debt in the past. If the problem is a liquidity crunch, short-term exposures may end up as long-term debt after a restructuring is completed, while term exposures may be spared any generalized debt relief procedures. That was the case in Korea's 1997-98 financial crisis. Special care should also be taken with short-term bridge loans that are meant to be taken out by capital market issues. The bridge may be a bridge to nowhere, and 'short-term exposure may turn out to be unanticipated term debt.

Bonds are another area where the unexpected may occur. Bonds have generally been omitted from debt restructurings for a number of reasons. Historically, widespread ownership of bonds has meant that the problems of identifying the owners of bonds and bringing them into restructuring negotiations effectively exempted bonds from country risk problems. That may no longer be the case. Modern information systems are capable of doing a far better job of identifying bondholders today than in the past. Equally, if not more important, is the increasingly aggressive stance being taken by the IMF and industrial country governments about equal sharing of pain among all creditors when generalized debt restructuring occurs. The argument is that it is not only more equitable, but will lead to more prudent lending.

Sizing Limits

There is no simple answer to the question of how large limits should be in countries where country risk is an issue, with one exception. That exception is where the risk is so substantial that no exposure should be contemplated. At the other end of the spectrum, there are a handful of advanced economies where country risk imposes no constraints on lending. These are the countries where financial markets are broad and deep, legal systems are sophisticated and enforcement is predictable. Credit and market risk may be substantial in these countries, but country risk is not an issue. Country limits may be set for these countries nevertheless, but their major purpose is to impose discipline with regard to business plans and lending strategies.

The answer to what limits should be for the countries between the polar cases is not an easy one. A number of issues should be taken into account. Among them are the following:

- The country grade, i.e., the degree of country risk present.

- The risk appetite of the financial institution and the perceived risk-reward tradeoff in the country.

- Confidence in the ability to forecast economic and financial developments in the country.

- Aggregate limits will be related to the capital base of the lending institution. The relationship may be explicit, as in specified percent of capital, or the relationship may be less rigid. Capital is the ultimate source of protection against loss, and as such the capital base will constrain not just the limits in each country, but the aggregate cross-border limit as well.

- Opportunities for profitable business. This consideration will constrain the upper limit no matter how high the quality of the country. Limits that exceed the scope of business envisioned in the strategic business plan are an invitation to undertake exposures beyond the prudent capacities of the lender to manage. This means that high-quality small countries where profitable business opportunities are limited may have smaller limits than larger but lower quality countries.

Just as with country grades, limits once set are not immutable. The goal should be to set limits with the long term in mind, but limits should be subject to annual renewal and review. However, the country risk system should be flexible enough to review and change limits as often as circumstances dictate.

In theory, the sum of the individual exposure categories equals the credit limit for the country. But simple addition of exposure categories that carry different degrees of risk will not provide a picture of aggregate risk. Risk mitigated exposures such as future flow transactions represent lower risk on a dollar-for-dollar basis than balance of payments loans to the sovereign. One answer to this problem is the assignment of exposure coefficients that vary according to the perception of risk. In practice it is difficult to assign coefficients on a valid basis. Another answer to this issue is to size different limit categories with the risk differentials in mind. When more experience has been gained with the behavior of different risk categories in country risk events, a valid statistical basis for assigning coefficients to exposure categories may emerge.

Location of Risk

There are mitigants to country risk that can shift the country of risk from the country where the exposure is located to another country where the quality of country risk is higher. Some of these devices may inadvertently shift the location of exposure to a country where the risk is considered greater. Parent company guarantees, for example, may have this effect.

The general rule that determines the country of risk states that the risk is located where the primary means of servicing the debt is located. Two commonly used risk mitigants are guarantees and collateral. A guaranteed exposure shifts the risk to the country where the guarantor is located. This is the country of ultimate risk. The same is true for collateral. The country of risk is the one in which the collateral is controlled. The general rule applies to other areas where assigning the country of risk is problematic, such as with shipping exposures.

The Country Review

The country review is the mechanism that brings all of the components of the country risk management system together. The purpose of the country review is to examine the economic and political environment in each country where cross-border exposures exist or are planned, to confirm the country grade or establish a new one, to review existing exposures and to set limits that will be valid over the coming year.

It is important that the key individuals responsible for creating and managing the exposures in the country attend the country review. The country review not only provides key decisions about the activities and risks that will be undertaken in a country, it is also a time when knowledge of the risks and rewards relating to the country is enhanced.

Large financial institutions with cross-border exposure in numerous countries will normally review countries in regional groupings. This is appropriate not only because of the regional management organizations in the institutions, but also because a country's performance can be put in perspective relative to others in its regional grouping.

The country review on a regional basis should be held annually. Individual countries should be reviewed as often as events dictate.

The goal of the country review is not just to set the mechanical parameters for business, but to develop consensus about the risks and rewards related to that business. The development of consensus as it arises out of discussion of the various aspects of country risk goes far toward managing those risks.

Monitoring Country Risk

Finally, good country risk management requires the monitoring of events in countries on a regular basis. The monitoring should track not only economic and political developments in the country and region, but existing exposures. For large financial institutions, that involves the creation and maintenance of sophisticated information systems that can adjust exposure to account for such risk mitigants as guarantees and collateral. The development and installation of information systems is critical for country risk management.

Country risk analysis can do little to reduce the volatility that has been made possible by modern information and communication systems. But it can help minimize the adverse impact of that volatility by helping to distinguish between those countries in which crises caused by volatile capital flows and exchange rates will lead to economic breakdowns and those that are fundamentally sound and will recover quickly. It should not be asked to do more.

Graph 1

1997 DEBT SERVICE/EXPORTS COMPARED

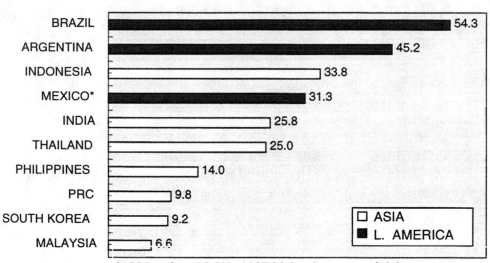

*1998 ratio = 22.0%; 1997 higher because of debt prepayments

Graph 2

1997 RESERVES/SHORT-TERM DEBT COMPARED

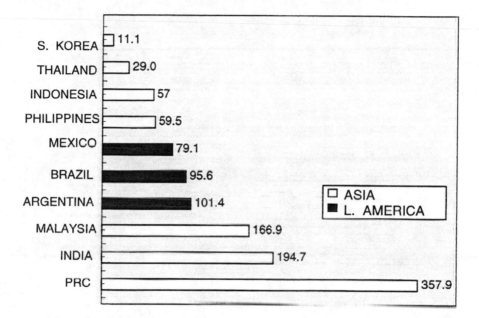

Graph 3

1997 RESERVES/DEBT SERVICE COMPARED

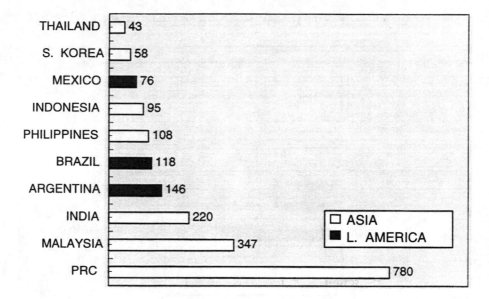

Chapter 8

Planning to Deal with Risk: A Case Study*
William E. Dugan

Case Background

In its initial foray into international operations, MilWood Products Inc. embarked on subsidiary operations in Latin America. The decision was based on the progression of the company's years of growth. Headquartered in the upper Midwest, MilWood had secured the lion's share of the fabricated wood products market in North America. A diversified network of production centers enabled the company to bring its product to market in a more timely fashion than the competition, and regional distribution outlets were able to fill contractor orders in days rather than weeks. Growing demand for their products throughout South America prompted the company's decision to explore subsidiary operations in the region.

MilWood executives participated in fact finding missions to various countries, initiated market research and feasibility studies, examined transport networks and researched the availability of a skilled workforce. Working through the Ex-Im Bank, they also addressed host country fiscal and monetary policy risk, exchange rate systems and regulatory policy. The MilWood team then met with foreign government officials and discussed collective bargaining agreements with local labor leaders. Satisfied with their findings, company executives made the decision to invest in a production and distribution facility designed to meet projected regional demand over the next decade.

Despite initial success, however, MilWood Products S.A. failed to achieve the envision return on investment. The problem was not related to the management structure of the foreign operation nor inaccurate projections of demand. Instead, in its initial risk assessment, the company failed to anticipate the host country's

---

* This chapter was originally published as William E. Dugan, "Global Dangers: Political Risk Part I," *Risk Management*, September 1999. It is reprinted with permission from *Risk Management* magazine. Copyright 1999 RMSP, Inc. All rights reserved.

legislative agenda. The broader political and economic conditions that had been so attractive to MilWood—the government's emphasis on privatization and liberalization (deregulation), property rights of foreign investors and a stable exchange rate system—generated political demands from competing interests.

Within eighteen months of MilWood's foreign start-up, the labor code of the host country was revised. The old code dated to the 1930s, reflecting the political and economic conditions of that period; the revised legislation was defined by the global climate of the new millennium. The emphasis on controlling labor through co-optive and repressive means was replaced by broader worker rights and a decreased role for government.

Whereas the subsequently altered labor-management relations ultimately contributed to slight increases in MilWood's production costs, the company's transportation costs doubled. The old labor code reflected the government's response to violent rail union activity in the 1930s; it provided for tight control of these organizations, including a restrictive wage regime. The revised code removed these restrictions, allowing market forces to determine wage and price structures in the transportation industry—both increased. The outcome was a shrinking bottom line for MilWood Products S.A.

While the MilWood scenario is hypothetical, it is based on a composite of cases and events that captures the essence of political risk assessment. In this case, it seemed that company executives had thoroughly analyzed the business risks associated with overseas investment. These decision makers, however, had little knowledge of the host country's labor history. Furthermore, they failed to project the macro level impact of the government's development program (privatization and liberalization) on diverse sectors of society. Given these limitations, MilWood executives could not have anticipated the increased cost of operation resulting from the transformation of the broader political landscape.

Foreign direct investment, particularly in the economies of the developing world, offers a wealth of opportunity. The risks associated with operations in unfamiliar and potentially hostile environment, however, are also greater. With the success or failure of overseas operations influenced by the actions of host governments and competing political actors, political risk management has become an essential component of any profitable foreign investment strategy.

Identifying Political Risk

The field of political risk assessment boasts a voluminous literature defining the theoretical parameters of the concept and methods of analysis. For our purposes, however, political risk can be addressed in terms of three broad categories that illustrate its scope.

The first, *catastrophic events*, includes political developments that can affect the operations of all foreign firms in a country. These events include racial and ethnic discord, civil strife, terrorism, civil war, international conflict and systemic failure. The common denominator is politically related violence. These events are less common than other forms of political risk, yet the impact can be devastating.

The civil strife that enveloped Indonesia in 1998, culminating in the downfall of the Suharto government, caused extensive damage to the physical infrastructure of foreign entities and resulted in billions of dollars of lost revenue. The ethnic discord, civil war and international conflict that has engulfed the former Yugoslavia has crippled foreign operations in these states. Terrorist activity (bombings and kidnapping and assassinations of executives) around the globe has resulted in tragedy for numerous foreign enterprises.

The second category, *business environment*, includes risks related to government corruption, labor strife, elections and the judicial system. The risks associated with this category may apply to the operations of all foreign companies in a given country or they may be industry, firm, or project specific. For example, widespread corruption among customs officials may impact the export/import operations of all foreign firms. On the other hand, some companies may receive preferential treatment, to the detriment of competitors, for "services rendered." In some sectors, projects may be awarded not to the lowest bidder, but to the firm willing to "enhance" the standard of living of a government minister.

For most U.S.-based companies, labor relations generally entail collective bargaining agreements that focus on issues of compensation, benefits and working conditions. In overseas environments, however, political issues are frequently added to the mix. Throughout Latin America, labor confederations generally maintain close affiliations with political parties. Functioning as political agents, these organizations commonly support party platforms or the activities of affiliate interests. As the vanguard of interests opposing government policy, labor confederations occasionally call for *general strikes* that close businesses nationwide. Despite amicable relations with its workforce, the foreign enterprise is exposed to losses associated with such a work stoppage.

Elections serve as an intervening variable in the construction of risk scenarios. This political process generally does not impact foreign operations directly, but rather through shifts in public policy. A new administration may take a wholly different approach to foreign investment than its predecessor, thus altering the business climate for all foreign operations; or it may limit its initiatives to a specific economic sector in the form of regulatory policy or tax reform. Conversely, elections and subsequent policy shifts may present opportunities to foreign investment rather than increased risk. In Argentina for example, the Menem administration (1989-99) initiated programs that transformed the forty-year-old protectionist, highly regulated, state-centered economy to a system characterized by decreased regulation, private enterprise and international competition.

The third category, *public policy*, overlaps business environment risks, as demonstrated above. Policy risk spans a broad range of political initiatives. It includes the mass expropriation of foreign assets, a policy decision usually associated with radical change in the political environment. While political events of this nature are extremely rare (e.g., Cuba, Chile, Ethiopia, Iran), the losses are considerable.

More common are risks associated with changes in tax systems, regulatory structure and monetary policy. The successive waves of economic crisis that have engulfed emerging markets over the past two years have forced foreign governments (the Asian Tigers, Russia and Brazil) to devalue currency, an approach that usually precipitates capital flight of liquid assets and additional rounds of devaluation. Such decisions are commonly accompanied by soaring interest rates intended to protect international reserves. High interest rates subsequently hamper domestic enterprise and alter consumer spending habits which, dependent upon the nature of foreign operations, can affect input or output. Shifts in monetary policy thus impact the bottom line both directly and indirectly.

Policy agendas are influenced by a broad set of political actors and myriad factors, both domestic and international. Host governments also pursue programs that contribute to changing policy vis-à-vis other sectors of society. In order to minimize political risk exposure, firms must be cognizant of the broad range of policy risk that can affect performance.

Managing the Risk

Organizational planning is fundamental to effective political risk management and should commence prior to investment decisions. This applies to companies entering the international arena for the first time as well as large multinationals expanding into new markets or ventures. *Pre-entry planning*, at a minimum, brings investment objectives into high relief, provides an indicator of the company's knowledge and expertise related to the proposed foreign environment, and integrates political risk assessment at an early stage. *Pre-investment planning* can also identify opportunities that benefit the company and circumvent risk. These include negotiated agreements with host governments on such issues as tax incentives, infrastructure and property rights.

The structure of operations is also established in the pre-investment stage. Some companies elect to develop in-house centers to gather, process and disseminate information. Others decide to outsource part of the risk assessment process to consulting firms with country, regional or global political risk expertise. These firms offer a host of services ranging from work on specific projects to long-term monitoring of political environments.

Development of strategy and contingency plans should begin in the pre-entry stage and continue throughout the lifespan of the investment. As an operative in a foreign country, the corporation becomes a political actor. Given this distinction, strategy should be formulated with respect to a range of initiatives, including governmental communication, public relations and the policy agenda. Contingency plans must also be developed (and modified as the political environment changes) to deal with catastrophic events. As these situations unfold, security issues are paramount: plans must be in place to provide for the protection or evacuation of personnel.

Insurance coverage is essential to overseas investment and should be incorporated into the pre-investment stage. Various options exist through private sector insurance companies, the U.S. government's Overseas Private Investment Corporation and international organizations such as the Multilateral Investment Guaranty Agency of the World Bank. OPIC pays claims on losses occurring from expropriation, inconvertibility and political violence (the latter being defined as loss of assets or income due to war, revolution, insurrection or politically motivated civil strife, terrorism and sabotage). Coverage is limited to U.S. businesses only. MIGA is available to U.S. and non-U.S. firms and offers coverage on losses associated with inconvertibility (the inability to convert local currency into foreign exchange and transfer it outside the country), expropriation, war and civil disturbance, and the breach or repudiation of a contract by the host government.

Catastrophic events capture the attention of the international business community. They result in loss of property, income and, tragically, human life. Property and income losses, however, can be recovered through insurance coverage. In the case of other types of political risk (the more common business environment and policy risks), the best insurance is organizational planning, a sound knowledge of the political environment and due diligence.

Chapter 9

The Resurgence of Political Risk Insurance[*]
Gerald T. West and Keith Martin

The crises which have occurred in Asia, Latin America, and Eastern Europe in the last two years have served to remind investors that political/economic events do not merely have a *potential* to cause losses, but actually *do*, on occasion, cause losses. The crises themselves, and the fact that they came as a surprise to many forecasters, have caused many investors to pay more careful attention to political risk assessment and management. Project sponsors are finding that to assemble the financing for new ventures, especially for large infrastructure projects, they must now look considerably more closely at political risk management issues.

Following a brief discussion of some macro factors currently affecting the market, there is an extended discussion in this paper of the renaissance in the investment insurance marketplace that has been underway for the last several years. A concluding section discusses trends for the future.

Prospective investors have not previously enjoyed the breadth and depth of choices in the investment insurance market that they have today. Yet it is also clear that project developers have not fully appreciated, at either the strategic or technical levels, the alternatives they now have in designing and improving their overall project structures.

MACRO TRENDS

Several 1990s trends have had a profound impact on the political risk investment insurance market. Foremost is the dramatic rise of foreign direct investments (FDI) flows into developing countries. Globalization, liberalization and privatization served to increase FDI flows more than sixfold during the period from 1990 to 1999. FDI flows to developing countries as a percentage of total long-term flows also rose dramatically in this period, from 24 percent in 1990 to

---

[*] This is a revised and updated version of "Political Risk Investment Insurance: A Renaissance," by Gerald T. West (*Journal of Project Finance*: Summer 1999, pp. 27-36).

68 percent in 1999. At the same time, official development aid fell to 18 percent of overall flows.

As developing and emerging market countries competed to attract FDI and gain investor confidence, losses due to traditional political perils were rare. Investors suffered relatively few expropriation losses; currency transfer losses were equally low as most investment returns were modest and a significant repatriation of profits was not expected to occur until later in the decade. While losses due to war were increased somewhat over the period as the Cold War-enforced stability eroded and internal conflicts broke out in many countries (especially in Africa), the losses remained fairly small and confined to somewhat predictable places.

For political risk investment insurers, the dramatic increase in FDI flows during the period translated into a growing market with very modest losses (until the onset of claims arising from the Asian crisis). Figure 1 notes the collective coverages written by the 24 investment insurance members of the Berne Union.[1] However, it should also be noted that, relative to the total flow of FDI, the percentage of investment covered by the 24-member Berne Union investment insurers had been on a downward trend until 1998, when there was a slight increase (see Figure 2). While Figure 2 does not include the political risk coverages provided by private insurers, it is clear that many investors were either bearing the risk of loss themselves or using other risk mitigation instruments.

The future continues to look auspicious for political risk investment insurers. An anonymous 1999 survey of 152 investors[2] supports the conclusion that many investors are now more concerned about political risks than before, but do not believe they have adequate coverage for their projects or that current coverage options are insufficient. According to the survey, half of all investors stated that political risks were more of a concern for them now than before, while only 12 percent indicated that they were now of less concern. A significant number of investors (about a third) believe that only a "minority" of their political risks are mitigated by current insurance products, indicating that products currently available are not meeting their expectations. Finally, many investors plan to increase their spending on political risk insurance in the next five years, using a combination of public and private insurers, as well as other instruments (e.g., captive insurers and finite insurance, if available).

One interesting development in the wake of the financial crises has been the divergence between the capital markets and foreign direct investment. While FDI has continued increasing every year – even in 1997 and 1998, the main years of the crisis –reaching an all-time high of US$192 billion in 1999, international capital market flows (including bank lending and bond financing) have largely collapsed. In 1996, those capital market flows peaked at US$151.3 billion, but have since fallen to US$46.7 billion in 1999 (which is less than half of their 1998 levels). The Russian debt moratorium in October 1998 dramatically reduced investor interest in emerging markets' equity issues; many Russian bonds were downgraded to "junk status." Equity prices in 12 out the 15 major emerging stock markets plunged (with a range of 21 to 85 percent); some of these markets, with the notable exception of Russia, have subsequently recovered most or all of those losses. For most middle income developing countries, however, access to the international capital and derivatives markets remains restricted, and maturities are shorter.

While some of this weakness in the capital markets is attributable to the continued strength of the developed economies, and of the United States in particular, the source resides primarily in the capital markets investors' continued nervousness about long-term future political and economic developments in emerging markets. In this context, the political risk insurance coverage for capital markets transactions that is currently being pioneered by OPIC, MIGA and Zurich-US (see below) may prove to be a small, but important, catalyst to stimulating capital markets financing for projects in developing countries.

Figure 1
Investment Insurance Provided by Berne Union Members

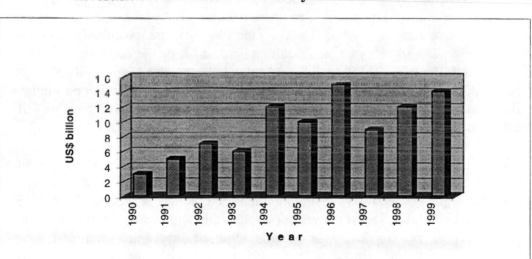

Source: 2000 Annual Report of the Berne Union.

Figure 2
Ratio of FDI Covered by Berne Union Investment Insurers to Foreign Direct Investment Flows

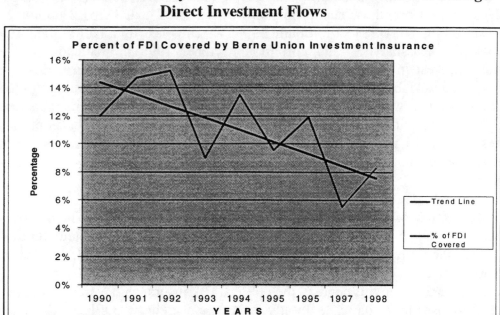

Sources: Global Development Finance 1998 and 1999; 1999 Annual Report of the Berne Union.

As investors assess the array of investment opportunities in developing markets today, they are far more wary than they were in the mid-1990s. The previously rosy international investment perspective that drove the demand for capital markets and derivatives products has turned pessimistic, and many prospective investors are sitting on the sidelines, despite promising signs of economic recovery in many of the countries hardest hit by the crisis (e.g., Korea, Malaysia and Brazil). This has led to a split between those engaged in direct investment, who continue to actively explore the significant opportunities available in developing countries – and those in the capital markets, who are still focusing on the potential for financial instability in emerging markets.

Clearly, there are countries and sectors which were hard hit by the 1997-1998 crises and have not recovered. Where losses have materialized and a country shows few signs of recovery, disillusionment is evident. Investors have been more attentive to their prospective ability to earn and repatriate profits; the necessary legal and regulatory safeguards required for capital and derivative markets to operate efficiently in many emerging economies are being more carefully assessed; and the effects of the credit crunch on the availability and cost of capital for limited recourse projects is very evident.

Overview of the Investment Insurance Market

While modestly growing in the 1990's, many political risk insurers were also quietly improving and redesigning their coverages and increasing their capacity. As late as 1997, the three main groups of investment insurers largely served separate markets and had clearly defined roles (see Figure 3). For new investments, national agencies dominated the market due to the length of their tenor, the scope of their coverage and their available capacity; private insurers served investors whose investments were not eligible for coverage from national providers and those with special needs. Multilateral insurers complemented the capacities of these two groups, especially with respect to investments that would not be eligible for coverage from national agencies, contributing capacity to very large investments and to special projects in transition economies and the poorest countries.

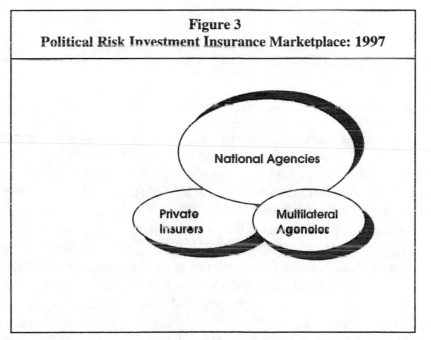

Figure 3
Political Risk Investment Insurance Marketplace: 1997

A different market has now emerged (see Figure 4). It is a larger, more complex and competitive marketplace. New companies backed by significant capital, such as Sovereign, Chubb & Son, and Zurich-US, entered the market. Also, private insurers dramatically improved the quality and tenor of their offerings. Although it seemed in 1998 that the effects of the Asian crisis (and of some of the losses incurred there and in Russia) would curtail the availability and

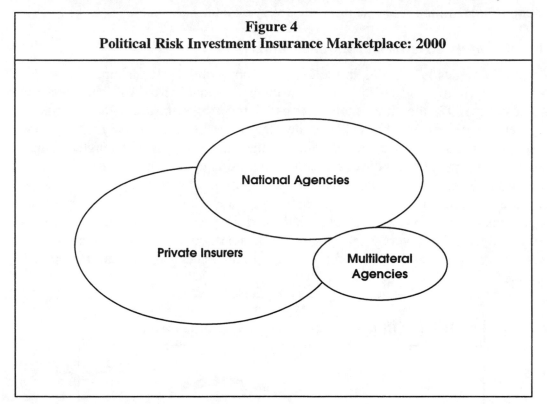

Figure 4
Political Risk Investment Insurance Marketplace: 2000

National Agencies

Private Insurers

Multilateral Agencies

amounts of private insurance capacity that can be accessed by investors, this has not yet happened. Capacity and rates in the private market appear to have remained stable, with only a moderate hardening of the reinsurance market taking place. The strong reinsurance market is, to a significant extent, supporting the long-term political risk coverages underwritten by both private and public providers. While many private insurers (and some public insurers) are now facing major claims, or have already paid claims, from their existing exposures in Indonesia, Russia, and Pakistan, this does not appear to have deterred the private insurers. Some are even pointing out that the claims payments had served to remind clients both that political risks are real and that insurers do pay valid claims. There is some debate about what the claims have meant for cooperation between public and private sector providers. On the one hand, the claims may underscore the value to private insurers of coinsurance with a public insurer, since there is a better chance that some of the losses will be recouped due to the public insurer's efforts[3]. On the other hand, a few private insurers have complained that public insurers are making claims determinations and recovery efforts subject to political considerations regarding the relationship between the public insurers' home country and the host country that has caused the claim.

Before describing the new developments in this market in more detail, and venturing some observations about future trends, it is useful to briefly comment on the utility of investment insurance as a risk management instrument.

The Utility of Political Risk Insurance in Risk Management

The intrinsic benefits of purchasing political risk insurance have been detailed elsewhere.[4] However, some benefits are worthy of particular note. Both debt and equity investors obviously recognize the compensatory value of investment insurance, but they often pay inadequate attention to two other important risk mitigation features: *deterrence and leverage*. This is especially the case in limited recourse financings.

Deterrence Value

The role of an investment insurer in the *settlement of investment disputes* is rarely discussed, much less analyzed. Political risk insurance, especially from national and multilateral agencies, can act as an effective deterrent against host government interference with insured private investments. Moreover, should an expropriation or currency transfer dispute occur, buyers clearly believe that, *ceteris paribus*, the investor stands a much better chance of successfully resolving the matter if a national or multilateral agency is involved as an insurer. (This thesis is clearly being "empirically-tested" in East Asia; the results so far are mixed.)

One can observe both "carrot" and "stick" aspects to this deterrent effect. First, with respect to the "carrot," one must remember that there is often a complex web of political, economic and commercial relationships between the investor's "home" country and the host developing country. These relationships are endangered by a messy dispute or claim involving their national insurer. Moreover, bilateral trade and investment treaties may be potentially violated; national security arrangements (actual or pending) may be threatened or inhibited; and on-going trade discussions may be disrupted. All these actions have real and reputational costs to the host country. Moreover, if the host country is undergoing a severe economic downturn, where can this country turn to obtain credits or loans other than the industrialized countries, or to the multilateral development institutions where the industrialized countries have significant influence? Finally, if the host country wishes to attract new foreign investment, it ironically needs these national investment insurers (and the multilateral insurers), who need to be prepared to issue new coverages (which they would obviously not do while dealing with a serious investment dispute or actively seeking compensation from the host government for a loss).

There are also some components of this deterrent effect that serve as a "stick," to be used against host countries which cause losses to national insurers and do not reimburse them. Some home countries have, by legislation or practice, introduced nearly automatic sanctions against countries which have not effectively compensated their national insurers who have assumed (through subrogation) the rights to an insured investor's assets or shares (in the case of expropriation claim) or to the local currency (in the case of a currency transfer claim). These sanctions can range from temporary suspension of a specific government program to complete cessation of all investment insurance, export credit and foreign assistance. Moreover, in the case of a dispute or claim with a multilateral insurer or guarantor which is not resolved, there is the risk of a complete suspension of on-going credit or loan activity (e.g., in the case of MIGA, a member of the World Bank Group, possible suspension of new IDA credits or IBRD loans).

Thus, considering all the "costs" associated with not satisfactorily resolving a dispute with an investor insured by a major national or multilateral insurer, a host country decision-maker certainly has many incentives (and disincentives) to carefully weigh before taking a prospective action against an insured investor. Indeed, once the full cost of prospective action against an insured investor is realized, these disputes often become "misunderstandings" which are quietly and successfully resolved.

It is difficult to label a specific government action (or inaction) as something that resulted from deterrence when such an action may well also be termed "enlightened self-interest". Such actions can be very narrow – and might be attributable to other factors. For example, the Russian Directive of August 26, 1998, which introduced temporary restrictions on residents' operations involving capital movements caused widespread concern among investors. However, the projects insured by MIGA were excluded from these restrictions by way of Article 8.1 of that Directive. Whatever the government motivation for this action was, the MIGA-insured investors in Russia were pleased with the exemption.

Direct evidence that deterrence has taken place is difficult to verify. In MIGA's case, the issuance of over 450 guarantees in more than 70 countries between 1990 and 2000, and the receipt of just one claim suggests deterrence was operative in some instances, since good underwriting cannot, by itself, justify such a record.

For many investors, the deterrence value is one of the prime reasons why they purchase insurance from public insurers, or at least insist on their involvement in the project. A further recognition of the value of this deterrence phenomenon is the fact that some project sponsors will deliberately involve multiple public and multilateral insurers and lenders in the same project, even when efficiency would argue for fewer participants.

Leverage Value

The second benefit of investment insurance that is often not acknowledged is leverage. Many lending institutions who underwrite debt in limited recourse project financings are also regular buyers of political risk investment insurance. Many of these OECD commercial bank investors are subject to very strict provisioning requirements with regard to their cross-border exposures.[5] To offset any further squeeze on the projects' economics brought about by these provisioning requirements, lenders often purchase political risk insurance from national or multilateral providers. (Such coverages then allow a lender to either eliminate or significantly reduce country risk provisioning requirements.)

Lenders also value political risk insurance for its ability to improve the overall risk/return profile of the project. Such insurance, often offered at attractive rates and tenors by insurers, allows lenders to extend the terms of their loans and thus improve the project's amortization profile.

These deterrence and leverage effects are added features that make political risk insurance a more attractive risk management mechanism in today's more difficult market for project finance. Figure 5 illustrates these features.

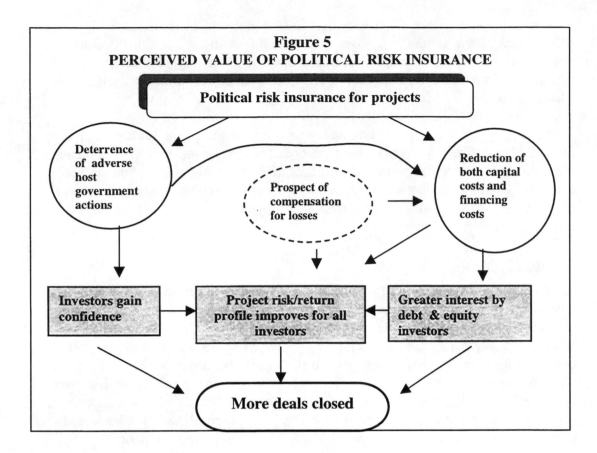

Figure 5
PERCEIVED VALUE OF POLITICAL RISK INSURANCE

A 1998 survey of all MIGA's clients (conducted on a confidential basis by an independent consultant for MIGA) revealed that they have diverse goals in mind when purchasing MIGA coverage. Some investors clearly value compensation against potential losses as much more important than the benefits of deterrence. Conversely, investors who value investment insurance's deterrent effect tend to minimize the importance of the compensation benefit, though this clearly does not mean that these investors do not expect to be compensated in the event of a loss. Over three-quarters of those respondents who valued the deterrent effect more than the compensation benefit also ranked MIGA's coverage as absolutely critical to their decision to proceed with the investment.

Since MIGA's clients are only a small proportion of all investors using investment insurance, one can not generalize to the larger universe of all investors. However, the results of the survey provide insight into investors' concerns and how the political risk insurance market can respond to the varying needs of investors. Currently, the market is better able than ever before to provide investors with whatever they require -- be it deterrence, greater capacity, long term coverage, and complementarity with other risk mitigating instruments.

NEW DEVELOPMENTS AND FUTURE CHALLENGES

It is useful to separate factors which will affect the political risk investment insurance marketplace into those which primarily impact the future demand for coverage, and those which will impact the future supply of coverage.

Demand Factors

The 1997 East Asian financial crisis and its aftermath have provided investors with a very concrete reminder that political risk is not "dead or irrelevant" as some had confidently announced a few years ago. Political risks have a history of simply "mutating" and presenting different management challenges to investors.

There are several factors that will fuel the demand for political risk insurance in the medium term. First, while demand for infrastructure financing has temporarily slackened, demand for investment insurance of such financings has increased. For example, MIGA gross issuance of new political risk insurance coverage for infrastructure projects increased from $228.7 million in fiscal year 1999 to $748.6 million in fiscal year 2000. This also reflects the fact that many large infrastructure projects in emerging countries were not been cancelled, but postponed until the economies began recovering and the cost/availability of capital began to improve. In many emerging markets, however, that recovery has yet to begin, so it is doubtful that demand for coverage of infrastructure projects has peaked already.

Secondly, while the new project pipeline has contracted in Asia, the demand for corporate restructuring, particularly merger and acquisitions, is expected to push up demand for financing in the region. In the five Asian countries most affected by the crisis, participation by foreign investors in merger and acquisition activities increased from $1.1 billion in 1996 to nearly $6 billion in 1997[6]. By 1999, overall FDI to 3 of those 5 countries (Malaysia, Philippines and Thailand) had reached near-record levels. In Korea, FDI reached US$8 billion in 1999, the largest amount ever, and a 250% increase over 1997 levels. In all of these cases, mergers and acquisitions accounted for much of the activity.[7]

Interestingly, while public investment insurers were expecting significant amounts of coverage to be written for projects in these East Asian countries, this has, by and large, not materialized. There are several plausible explanations for this. In the case of Malaysia and Korea, the fact that few, if any, political risk insurance losses were suffered during the crisis, coupled with the rapidity and depth of the economic recovery in both countries, appears to have persuaded investors to return to those countries without political risk coverage. In the Philippines, investors – particularly in the power sector – remain nervous about sufficient consumer demand to support the current pipeline of large-scale infrastructure projects. This means that a number of investors have chosen not to go forward with new projects, and hence do not require political risk coverage. Only in Thailand have investment insurers seen a certain measure of interest for coverage of new projects.

In Indonesia, both investors and investment insurers are waiting for clarification of the situation. A number of investment insurers, including OPIC and several Lloyd's syndicates, have now paid substantial claims to insured investors whose projects in Indonesia's power sector were adversely impacted by the economic and political turmoil in the country. OPIC's claims payment of US$217.5 million was one of the largest in its history. MIGA paid out its first claim, for $15 million, in June 2000, for a power project in Indonesia.

On the qualitative side, demand for investment insurance will also be driven by the resurgence of classical political risk as a result of the social dislocation and political turmoil brought about by the economic crisis. While no government has engaged in wholesale expropriation for nearly two decades, the possibility of selective expropriations is higher than ever in some countries, due to rising nationalism. Mergers and acquisitions in East Asia have fueled some nationalistic paranoia among both government and business elites, who fear that foreigners are conspiring to buy into local companies at "fire-sale" prices to gain dominance over their economy. Similarly, where privatizations involving heavy foreign participation have resulted in layoffs, increased rates for basic services, or a deterioration in the quality of those services, protests have happened and can be expected to include calls for nationalization or result in violent attacks on the company's facilities. Finally, expropriation and civil war risks are obviously higher in countries where the government has been weakened and society is divided by differences.

Civil wars and general chaos in several African countries – combined with a desire on the part of some investors to tap into the continent's markets and resources – have fueled demand for investment insurance in Africa. Demand for coverage is highest in those African countries emerging from crises but which have good business prospects (e.g., Mozambique). While this demand remains very modest when compared to Latin America, it is an encouraging sign that MIGA was able to substantially increase coverage for projects in Africa in fiscal year 2000; they now represent 12% of MIGA's entire portfolio. The concern for investment insurers, however, is that the risk of civil strife is probably the highest risk facing their investments in Africa – and it is the one risk for which there is virtually no opportunity for recoveries once a claim has been paid.

In addition to these classical political risks, investors also face more economic uncertainties. Many forecasters and international institutions are predicting that global economic growth will continue at a modest pace for the next few years; this will hamper the efforts of most developing countries to raise capital. Currency exchange volatility will impede the ability of investors to service their foreign currency debts and purchase needed imports. Large-scale movements of currency may also result in some countries' inability to maintain sufficient foreign currency reserves, hence leading to a currency crisis. Many investors will continue to suffer from business volatility arising from erosion of their customer base, vulnerability to regional uncertainties, selective discrimination, cancellation of operating and export licenses, and contract abrogation. Because of the breadth and depth of these kinds of uncertainties, limited recourse investors are likely to be heavy purchasers of political risk investment insurance in the next few years.

Supply Factors

The demand "pull" for investment insurance in the 1990's stimulated competition and innovation and has been paralleled in some respects by a supply "push". Some of this push was fueled by the soft insurance market, as private underwriters sought better margins in market niches where competition has not driven premiums to low levels. In some instances, existing investment insurance providers seem to have dramatically improved their coverage offerings to maintain existing market share, and meet increased demand. Some private entrants seem to be entering the political risk market just to keep pace with their competition and be a "full service" insurer to their clients.

It is useful to discuss four aspects of the changing investment insurance market in more detail: capacity, tenor, innovation, and cooperation/collaboration among insurers.

Capacity:

During the last two years, private insurers have responded to the increased demand stimulated by recent economic and political uncertainties in developing countries by increasing their classic confiscation, expropriation, nationalization (CEN) capacity per project by an estimated 14 percent (from an estimated $1.4 billion in 1998, to $1.6 billion in 1999)[8]. Lloyd's of London still accounts for a large share of this increase; its CEN capacity in 1999 reached $900 million compared to $800 million during the previous year. It should be noted, however, that Lloyd's capacity is notoriously difficult to estimate for several reasons. First, the market measures itself in terms of premium that can be written, not capacity per se. Secondly, it depends very heavily on the availability and rates for reinsurance. Finally, both reinsurance and primary insurance capacity will often depend on events in totally unrelated lines of the insurance business.

On the last two points, it is worth noting that, historically, the general insurance business has been cyclical, with periods of low losses (and high profits) counterbalanced by times of high insurance losses. When losses occur, capacity may dry up not only in the specific sector affected, but in altogether different lines as well (since reinsurers usually cover a variety of lines of insurance). The private insurance market is currently coming out of one of the longest cycles of low losses in its history, and many have predicted that the end of the cycle (and, hence, higher losses) would result in increased premiums and decreased capacity. At the same time, however, large amounts of capital have flowed into the insurance industry from a variety of sources, resulting in both increased capacity and historically low premium rates. There is, therefore, a significant fear that, at some point, large losses totally unrelated to political risks, e.g. due to a particularly damaging hurricane season, will affect the political risk insurance market and result in a withdrawal of capacity and/or significantly higher premium rates in the private political risk insurance industry. As a consequence, there will always be a latent concern about sudden swings in private political risk insurance capacity among investors. In sum, both overall investment insurance capacity and capacity for any given risk in a particular country are volatile for a variety of reasons over which private investment insurers have little control.

Figure 6 below gives a more detailed perspective of the available capacity of private insurers per project, showing additional capacity coming from Lloyd's, Zurich-US, and a composite group of other private insurers.

Figure 6
CEN Per Project Capacity of Selected Private Insurers

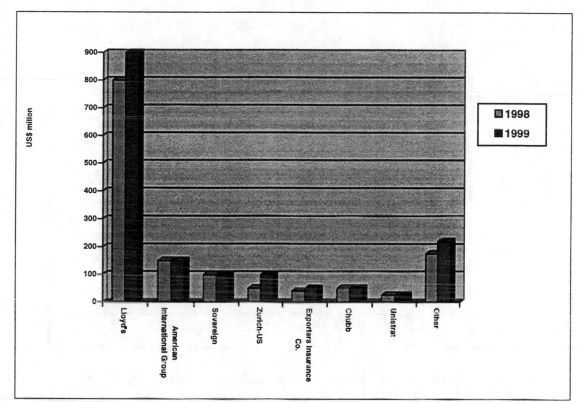

Source: Berry, Palmer & Lyle, May 1999.

Collectively, the national insurers have expanded their issuance of investment insurance significantly in the 1990's. New coverage issued by Berne Union members (which encompasses 24 national investment insurers and MIGA) rose dramatically in the 1990's. Their total portfolio at December 31, 1998, was about US$42 billion, an increase of 62% over 1992 levels. Berne Union members' coverage is expected to stay near, or even exceed, these record levels as individual OECD governments announce special initiatives to support various special recovery initiatives and as investors in large, complex projects in the developing world continue to seek the involvement of public insurers. Furthermore, the recent addition of AIG to the Berne Union will automatically increase those figures.

With respect to capacity limits, official agencies have also demonstrated considerable flexibility (see Table 1). Many national agencies are very "elastic" and can supply large amounts of coverage for projects deemed to be in the "national interest" because of procurement in the home country or for political reasons. (OPIC and MIGA, with their per-project limits of US$200 million, are the exception, though those limits could be revised.)

Table 1
Limits of Some Public and Private Investment Insurers
(as of May 1999)

Investment Insurer	Country Limits (in US$ millions)	Project Limits (in US$ millions)
AIG	1,000 (higher in certain countries)	150
Sovereign	250	100
Zurich-US	300-1,000	100
Chubb	100	50
OPIC	about 1,800 (15% of insurance outstanding)	200
EDC	Variable	No official limit. (But about 100)
MIGA	up to 620	up to 200
ECGD	Variable	Variable

The supply push has resulted in a situation that makes it theoretically possible for nearly US$2 billion of capacity (from both public and private sources) to be mobilized for a single project. However, with respect to very large projects (more than US$1 billion), or projects considered more "risky", a common situation often arises, namely that the combined capabilities of all interested insurers may well fall short of investors' coverage requirements. However, from the perspective of the investment insurers, the demand seems to have become increasingly "lumpy", with heavy demand for large amounts of coverage in a relatively small number of projects, sectors and countries. In mid-2000, for example, demand for coverage of infrastructure projects in Brazil clearly exceeds available coverage.

Longer Tenor:

While the national agencies have always provided long term coverage (up to 15-20 years has been the norm), the tenor offered by private insurers had been essentially limited to 1 - 3 years until 1996. As Figure 7 notes, by mid-1999 this had dramatically changed and 10 year coverages are common. Two recent developments suggest that further improvements are likely. First, ACE Global Markets, one of the largest managing agency groups at Lloyd's of London, agreed in April 1999 to facultatively reinsure MIGA for its coverage of a mortgage lending project in Argentina; the tenor was 15 years. Second, in May 1999, Zurich-US announced that its maximum tenor had been extended from 10 to 15 years. Although the amount and availability of coverage may be limited for some investments, these actions suggest that the trend toward more capacity for longer tenors is likely to continue, barring unforeseen losses either in the political risk insurance industry or in unrelated lines (see above).

While availability and cost may continue to inhibit utilization of this extension of tenor, it is clear that project developers may not yet have fully appreciated the added flexibility they now have in designing and improving their overall project structures.

Figure 7
Maximum Tenor Offered by Selected Private Insurers in 1999

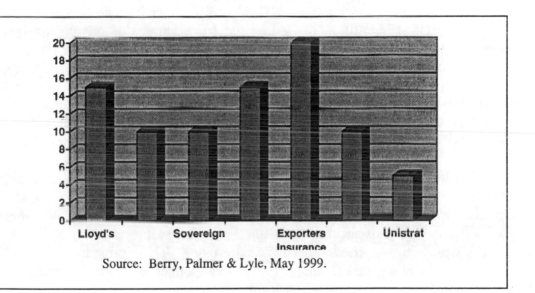

Source: Berry, Palmer & Lyle, May 1999.

It is also often overlooked that the longer tenor now offered in the combined public-private market can also help project sponsors access the secondary bond market. Securitized project bonds can be made more attractive to portfolio investors if they are backed by political risk insurance. CS First Boston (CSFB), for example, has started pooling senior secured project finance loans, of which twenty percent of the portfolio are rated non-investment grade, but are backed by political risk insurance.[9] Indeed, a number of securitizations in "difficult" markets would not happen without support from the investment insurance market.

Product Innovation:

The combination of heightened demand, increased capacity, competition, and longer tenor of coverage has stimulated innovation in the last few years, as has the growing complexity of the investments to be covered. Nearly every month witnesses a new coverage "wrinkle" or combination that has never been previously accomplished. Several recent examples can be noted.

• **BCP/Brazil:** In April 2000, MIGA signed its largest guarantee to date, supporting US$230 million of a $650 million loan from a syndicate of lenders to BCP in Brazil. In taking on the US$230 million coverage against transfer restriction and expropriation, MIGA utilized its Cooperative Underwriting Program (CUP – see below) and brought new partners into the CUP. MIGA is the insurer of record, but is only retaining US$55 million for its own account, with the remaining US$175 million being covered by a variety of private insurers (Chubb, Unistrat, and seven Lloyd's syndicates). The underlying project involves the establishment and operation of a cellular network in metropolitan Sao Paulo, providing improved telecommunications infrastructure in Brazil. This project demonstrates how effectively private and public insurers can work together to provide needed coverage in a very tight market, leveraging each other's advantages for the ultimate benefit of the investors and host country's economy.

• **Multicountry Pipelines:** A growing trend, especially in the power sector, is toward integrated multi-country projects which involve hydrocarbon or power production in one country and the transmission thereof to one or more other countries. Such projects are currently under way or in the planning stages in western Africa, Latin America and the Caspian region. These projects, which are often very large and expensive, are posing new challenges to investment insurers, who have traditionally dealt with political risks on a per-country basis. Demand from investors is, however, driving insurers to reassess the situation. In fiscal year 1999, for the first time, MIGA insured two gas pipeline projects with multi-country coverage, i.e. coverage against actions by the host government of one country that may affect the assets of the same project located either in the host country or in another country.

- In the first case, MIGA provided US$14.5 million in insurance for El Paso Energy International's investment in one of the largest foreign investments in Latin America, the construction of a 3150 km natural gas pipeline from Santa Cruz (Bolivia) to Porto Alegre (Brazil). The project will have direct economic benefits to the Bolivian economy through increased investment in upstream gas exploration and production activities, boosting the nation's income by an estimated US$400 million per annum. At the same time, the project will benefit Brazil by diversifying its energy supply and by substituting natural gas for more polluting fuels in the areas served by the pipeline.

- MIGA also issued US$31.4 million in coverage to EPED Holding Co. for its investment in a natural gas transmission project from Argentina to Chile. The project is part of an integrated energy project and will transmit natural gas from Argentina to Chile through the construction and operation of a 641 km pipeline. The natural gas will replace high-sulfur fuel oil, coal and firewood, alleviating pollution and deforestation in the areas of Chile using gas from the pipeline.

- **Creeping Expropriation and Breach of Contract Coverage:** In the context of investors' concerns that current coverage available from investment insurers is not adequate to protect them against all the risks they face, considerable attention is now being paid to "stretching" what can be covered under political risks This is also a reflection of the fact that privatizations, particularly in the infrastructure sector, have resulted in new situations where the line between political and commercial actions is becoming blurred, and where the role of parastatals and subsovereigns has made the accountability of the host country's central government less certain.

  - Of greatest concern to many investors today is "creeping expropriation," i.e. where a series of events by a government (or a subsovereign or parastatal entity) result in a deprivation of the investor's rights. While many public investment insurers want to accommodate investors' needs in this area, they often worry about the blurred distinction between commercial and political risks giving rise to claims for which they will find it difficult to recover from the host governments. This is an evolving area where cooperation between investors, private insurers and public insurers will be critical in developing better coverage that addresses investors' concerns without endangering the sustainability of public insurers and the profitability of private insurers.

  - With increasing numbers of privatizations, BOOT (Build-Own-Operate-Transfer) projects, and off-take agreements, investors and lenders have sought coverage from public insurers against breaches of host government commitments. Traditionally, public insurers have been reluctant to offer such breach of contract coverage, since these commitments often involve a gray area between political and commercial risk. (Private insurers, by contrast, have long offered contract frustration coverage, since they need not be as concerned about the distinction between commercial and political risks.) Over the past few years, however, due to the fact that their expropriation coverage may, on occasion, have included such coverage, public investment insurers have decided to clarify matters and respond to investor demand by offering more expansive and explicit breach of contract coverage. MIGA, for example, recently provided coverage for a buy-lease-back arrangement and maintenance agreements between a private company and the Lesotho government for some 1200 vehicles against specified breaches by the host government, a coverage that probably would have been unavailable from MIGA some years ago.

- **Coverage for Capital Markets Transactions:** In January 1999, OPIC announced its decision to provide political risk coverage of up to US$200 million per project of bonds (such as 144A bonds) issued in the US capital markets. This new product should facilitate limited-recourse projects in developing countries obtaining an investment-grade rating that may be higher than the country's sovereign rating and thereby enable them to access badly needed long-term financing. OPIC and Zurich-US have since covered several capital markets transactions, albeit for private placements, and MIGA is currently completing its first coverage for a Section 144A issue. It remains to be seen whether the coverage offered by investment insurers (who are only covering explicitly political risks) will be sufficient for investors in public placements, since many are concerned about devaluation risk and other commercial perils and are unaware of the full benefits of investment insurance. Other investors, particularly those who have done traditionally "higher risk" investments in developing markets, are primarily interested in the high yields these transactions offer and are concerned that the premium paid for political risk insurance will reduce the spread too much. In short, the capital markets coverage, while recognized by rating agencies, arrangers and others as a potentially very important catalyst for tapping the capital markets for developing country projects, is not a product that will meet the needs of all investors.

- **Banco Santander/Brazil:** In May 1999, MIGA issued coverage of $100 million of three-year notes from Banco Santander, S.A., of Spain to its wholly-owned Brazilian subsidiary to fund its lending activities. MIGA's contract, totaling $107 million in coverage, was coinsured under the CUP (see below) with Great Northern Insurance Company of the Chubb Group and with five Lloyd's syndicates. The transaction was noteworthy because it was the first issue of this tenor in Brazil since mid-1998.

While most of these innovations have been evolutionary in nature, rather than revolutionary, in the aggregate they have significantly improved the risk management options now available to project financiers.

Cooperation and Collaboration Among Investment Insurers:

Perhaps the most important development in the investment insurance marketplace in recent years is the increasing cooperation among investment insurers in large projects, especially infrastructure projects. For example, MIGA, which has a mandate to complement other investment insurers in facilitating investment into developing countries, has signed project reinsurance arrangements with British, Canadian, French, Japanese, Norwegian, and US national agencies. MIGA has also participated in coinsurance arrangements with a large number of private and public insurers. Such collaboration among insurers effectively increases the available insurance capacity for project developers and enhances the deterrent benefit for both insurers and insureds.

The long-term reinsurance arrangements which MIGA concluded in February 1999 with two Bermuda-based private insurance companies, ACE Insurance Company Limited (ACE) and XL Capital Limited (XL), show how an insurer can better serve the needs of prospective clients, augment its level of activity, and yet contain its own net exposure. The agreements build on an earlier agreement signed in April 1997 between MIGA and ACE. The key terms of these new reinsurance arrangements are:

- ACE and XL will each assume exposure of up to US$50 million per project and up to US$150 million per country; and
- MIGA will retain complete discretion as to its pricing policy and underwriting decisions.

As a result of these agreements, MIGA's per project and per country limits have increased substantially. With the infusion of US$150 million in capital in April 1998, plus an anticipated US$850 million over the next three years, MIGA's

Board of Directors approved in February 1999 an increase in its *net* per project limit from US$50 million to US$110 million and its *net* per country limit from US$250 million to US$350 million. The combination of expanded reinsurance and an increase in its per country and per project limits now allows MIGA to offer up to US$200 million of *gross* coverage to a single project, and a total of $620 million *gross* in a country. (Additional amounts of coverage can be mobilized through the CUP, facultative reinsurance with public and private insurers, as well as other forms of coinsurance.)

A recent example of this private-public sector cooperation is the reinsurance agreement that MIGA signed with the ACE Global Markets' Syndicate of Lloyd's of London covering a $50 million loan by Lloyds Bank of the UK to its wholly-owned subsidiary in Argentina. The loan will be used by the bank to expand its residential mortgage lending operations through Lloyds Bank's network of 51 offices in the country. The reinsurance agreement, with a maximum tenor of 15 years, allowed MIGA to provide additional coverage for the project which, in turn, enables Lloyds Bank to offer longer-term residential mortgages to its clients.

Another MIGA initiative which also reflects how public and private investment insurers may cooperate, is MIGA's Cooperative Underwriting Program ("CUP"). This is a mechanism which combines coverage from public and private insurers (up to US$300 million per project) in a manner similar to the IFC's "A" and "B" loan syndications. Under this arrangement, MIGA "fronts" the insurance for the private insurer(s) along with its own coverage, effectively sharing (for a price) its "status" as a multilateral entity and as a member of the World Bank Group.

A byproduct of the increasing cooperation among insurers is a trend toward the standardization of policy wordings. As private insurers increasingly cooperate with MIGA, EDC, and OPIC, they increasingly become accustomed to, and accept, the policy wordings of these agencies. This trend is likely to continue and become a standard for a number of reasons: buyer acceptance of their wordings; the openness of EDC, OPIC, and MIGA to cooperate with other insurers; and the prominence of these insurers in the marketplace.

CONCLUSIONS

Like all markets, the investment insurance market will be subject to many forces which will influence its future evolution. The difficult task is not so much to identify all these factors, but to consider their interactions and to *net* them out to determine the resultant magnitude and direction of the market. In that spirit, the authors offer the following observations:

- Stimulated by losses to uninsured investors, and notwithstanding stagnation in investment flows to developing and emerging markets, the issuance of political risk investment insurance will steadily increase, with specific growth in parts of Asia, the former Soviet Union, and Latin America. Issuance in Africa and the Middle East will also increase, but will remain a relatively small percentage overall.

- Due to increased losses, historically low premium rates in other insurance areas will not be sustainable over the longer term. Increased losses will result in a continued firming of rates. This will have some effect on the political risk investment insurance market as reinsurance capacity becomes more expensive.

- Notwithstanding some insurance losses in the political risk insurance area, capacity should remain fairly steady. Buyers should continue to benefit from competition among insurance providers and premium rates should remain relatively stable, albeit with an upward bias.

- Events in East Asia, the former Soviet Union and Latin America will result in sharper differences in the treatment afforded uninsured investments, and investments insured by private insurers versus those covered by national or multilateral providers. The value of deterrence should thus become more clearly established.

- Assembly of limited recourse debt financing for mega-infrastructure projects will be very difficult without long term investment insurance. Fortunately, cooperation and collaboration among insurers should continue to grow, especially with respect to such large projects.

- After the recent and dramatic increases in tenor in the private market (from 1-3 years to 10-15 years), there will be no further extensions in the near future and there will be greater price variation for tenor.

• As a result of significant losses in 1999 and 2000, insurers and reinsurers may reexamine their rates and their project and country limits. The result should be more variance across insurers, and hence a greater need for buyers to shop their insurance needs.

---

[1] The Berne Union was founded in 1934 with two main objectives: to promote international acceptance of sound principle in export credit insurance and investment insurance; and, the exchange of information relating thereto. The national and multilateral members of the Union's Investment Insurance Committee, currently numbering 24, provide investment insurance coverage against political risks. In 1999, AIG became the first private insurer writing coverage for its own account (not that of a national government) to join the Berne Union; it currently has Observer status but will be eligible, in 2001, to apply for full membership.

[2] While the survey was sponsored by MIGA, it was undertaken by an outside firm and respondents were unaware of any connection to MIGA.

[3] It is worth noting, for example, that OPIC has a record of recovering about 100% of the expropriation claims it has paid out, not including the recent claim paid in Indonesia.

[4] Gerald T. West "Managing Political Risk Insurance: The Role of Investment Insurance." *Journal of Project Finance*. Winter 1996, pp. 5-11.

[5] See, for example, Robert H. Malleck. "Political Risk Insurance, International Banks, and Other International Lenders" in Theodore H. Moran, ed. Managing International Political Risk. Blackwell Business. London. 1998. pp. 173-178.

[6] Global Development Finance 1999. The World Bank. Washington, D.C., p. 60.

[7] Global Development Finance 2000. The World Bank. Washington, D.C., p. 43.

[8] Source: Charles Berry's, Chairman of Berry Palmer & Lyle Limited, presentation on "Political Risk and Trade Credit Insurance From the Private Market," during the 9th Annual Insuring Export Credit and Political Risk Convention, London, February 10-12, 1999.

[9] Source: CS First Boston's presentation on Project Finance Loan Securitization, presented during the conference on New Solutions and Opportunities for Developing and Financing Projects. Paris, France, February 17-19, 1999.

Chapter 10

Insurance as Management[*]
Daniel Wagner

Abstract

In the shadows of worldwide political upheaval, the political risk insurance (PRI) marketplace has grown, expanding particularly in the latter 1990s to become more sophisticated in meeting the needs of global businesses. PRI has become an indispensable tool that bankers, equity providers and traders use to craft transactions. However, the buyer of PRI should beware. Plans to expand a business internationally easily can be derailed when a lender pulls the plug because PRI is no longer available. In the coming decade, the demand for PRI is unlikely to diminish. As political risks associated with international business increase with time, so will the value of using PRI to protect against them.

§ § §

Introduction

The world is a more dangerous place today than it was at the beginning of this decade. Although communism has breathed its last as a global force and democratization has spread throughout much of the world, the threat of terrorism has risen along with nuclear proliferation among rogue states. What has replaced the Cold War is an uneasy peace, where new challenges confront governments and international businesses at every curve. Yes, Mobutu is gone from the former Zaire, but he has been replaced by a seemingly endless cycle of political convulsions and violence in Central Africa. Suharto was ousted, but Indonesia, the fourth most populous nation on earth, is still plagued by anarchy in the streets and political and economic uncertainty. Jordan's King Hussein has been succeeded by his eldest son, but also by renewed uncertainty about the prospect of lasting peace in the Middle East. What will happen in Russia, Malaysia and Egypt when Yeltsin,

---

[*] This chapter was originally published as Daniel Wagner, "The Cluster Trend: Political Risk, Part II, Risk Management, September 1999. It is reprinted with permission from Risk Management magazine. Copyright 1999 RMSP, Inc. All rights reserved.

Mahathir and Mubarak step down? Then there is the question of the cost to be borne collectively by such changes in a world where markets never sleep and national livelihoods can depend upon the whims of currency traders.

In the shadows of worldwide political upheaval, the political risk insurance marketplace has grown. Particularly during the latter half of the 1990s, PRI has expanded and become more sophisticated to meet the needs of global businesses. At least three new major underwriters have been created since 1996, and others previously in the industry have returned. There are more brokers in the business than ever before and, likewise, reinsurers have stepped up to the plate, providing greater support for the burgeoning numbers of both public and private players.

The PRI market has also enhanced its ability to provide insurance for increasingly larger transactions, and developed new products to meet users' needs. Only five years ago, the maximum tenor for private sector investment insurance was just three years, with a maximum limit of liability of perhaps $500 million. Today, such insurance can cover up to ten years, with limits approaching $2 billion on a market-wide basis. It has become common for public sector underwriters (owned by governments) to work in tandem with private insurers to pool capacity. And it is now possible to insure a variety of financial instruments (such as bonds and letters of credit) that are frequently used in the everchanging world of global finance.

Exposure Problems

The result has been both exhilarating and problematic. PRI has become an indispensable tool that bankers, equity providers and traders use to craft transactions. For transactions in many developing countries, lenders will not dispense funds without it. But the insurance has been employed in so many trade and investment transactions that clusters of exposures have developed by country and sector. This is becoming an issue of concern for underwriters.

There are perhaps a dozen countries in the world where PRI capacity is either sold out or extremely limited, including Brazil, China and Russia. With so much new business in these areas, the sheer demand for the insurance explains the shortfall. Where demand is high, supply will dwindle. Also, the considerable perceived political risk implied in doing business in these countries further limits how much an insurer can safely write and how many insurance companies would consider the exposure for themselves. This makes PRI a very hot commodity.

Indeed, last year one insurer decided to auction off its remaining capacity in Brazil to the highest bidder. There was plenty of interest.

The demand for PRI for infrastructure projects has also resulted in clusters of exposures in places like Indonesia and Pakistan, where recent events have caused sleepless nights for underwriters.

The ousting of the Indonesian president and the dramatic swan dive of the rupiah left independent power producers (IPPs) in the region wondering if their power purchase agreements (PPAs) would be honored and whether the agreed-upon tariff rates would need to be changed. Under the circumstances, there was no way the Perusahaan Umurn Listrik Negara (the state-owned utility) could honor tariffs established when the rupiah was 2,500 to the dollar (it fell to as low as 17,000). The end result was that numerous claims were filed with underwriters in 1997 and 1998 for breach of contract and expropriation.

A similar story unfolded in Pakistan, where the Sharif government accused many IPPs of winning their contracts through bribery with the previous government of Benazir Bhutto (who was subsequently charged with corruption). At least a dozen foreign IPPs were put on notice that they would have to renegotiate their PPAs to reduce the tariff rates or face outright cancellation of the agreements. As in Indonesia, numerous claims for breach of contract and expropriation were filed.

Fortunately, in both cases many of these disputes were resolved during the waiting periods through negotiations between the IPPs and the governments. These events, however, point to a future risk: A crisis could arise if clusters of exposure result in numerous simultaneous claims that need to be paid.

As much as the PRI Industry has grown in the past five years, it remains a relatively small marketplace, generating correspondingly limited premiums. Given that claims in the recent past were worth hundreds of millions of dollars, it would not take much to upset the apple cart. Should many large claims materialize, reinsurers would undoubtedly withdraw or limit their support, causing the PRI marketplace to retrench rather rapidly, and per transaction and country limits to be severely reduced.

In fact, the PRI market has already suffered through such events. The last time, in the early 1990s, the impact was swift and dramatic. Reinsurance support dwindled and a number of syndicates at Lloyd's went out of business. Although most underwriters continued to operate, it took years for the market to build itself up again.

Although the insurance consumer continues to enjoy the benefits of a soft market, if the worst happens, and reinsurance support is curtailed for PRI providers as a result of catastrophic claims, the market will harden in no time at all

Managing the Risks

The buyer of PRI should beware. Plans to expand a business internationally can easily be derailed when a lender pulls the plug because PRI is no longer available.

To best protect your company's expansion strategy, start planning early in the investment process. Lock in PRI coverage during the initial stages of the project finance negotiations by paying a small commitment fee to the underwriters-money well spent for projects in countries where demand for PRI is high. Another good rule of thumb is to bring insurers into the negotiation process when loans are being arranged. Too often, PRI is addressed after a lending package has been finalized, when banks have already encumbered project assets. Insurers, who usually require pari passu treatment on this issue, are then left in the dust, and project sponsors must scramble to find an acceptable solution for the banks and the insurers. This often results in the sponsors losing out, as insurers may be forced to carve out coverage if a solution acceptable to all parties is not found.

Demand for PRI is unlikely to diminish in the coming decade. The world is only likely to become more dangerous for international businesses. Regardless, the lure of potential new markets will continue to attract investors and traders to the global business scene, where they will confront strange local laws, unfamiliar partners and fickle political climates. But with proper planning, even the impact of clusters of exposure need not affect a risk manager's ability to obtain and utilize PRI. The political risks associated with international business will grow with time, but so will the value of using PRI to protect against them.

Chapter 11

Dealing with Political Risk:
A Manager's Toolkit
Llewellyn D. Howell

Managerial Objectives in Political Risk Assessment

In planning a foreign investment in today's globalized and yet multifaceted system, the international manager has to become immediately aware of the general socio-political climate in which the investing firm must operate. Managers must first identify specific firm vulnerabilities, determine sources of risk that underlay them, and then match those vulnerabilities with attributes of the socio-political climate. Once these are identified, they must take the critical managerial step of applying the appropriate management tools to avoid, block, alter, or compensate for the sources of risk and possible losses to the investor. My purpose here is to walk through these stages, tying the existing and readily available means of assessment with proposed tools as a guide to managers who are facing increasing instances of political risk in rapidly emerging markets.

Country Level Assessments

There are many companies that provide political risk assessments as their product in this evolving global economy. Formal country and political risk assessments date to the 1960s, well prior to the period of the Iran debacle in which no governments or firms were really paying attention to assessments. What is now Business Environment Risk Intelligence (BERI) was originally "Business Risk Intelligence Information" and in the mid-1960s began its analysis of a limited number of countries, with a 10-variable 'political risk index'. The International Country Risk Guide (ICRG) began in an early format shortly thereafter. With several adjustments in structure, including the most recent in 1997, ICRG continues to provide a Country Risk assessment (political, financial, and economic risk) with its political risk index being the best known.

Both BERI and ICRG are attribute models that provide country-level analyses for all foreign investors in the host country, with what has come to be known as a "macro" analysis. By attribute models, I mean those risk forecasting models that rely on characteristics of the government or the society to determine some level of danger to foreign investors. Attribute models are in contrast to models such as that of Political Risk Services (PRS) that project central government decisions that might be adverse to foreign investors. Most models used in ratings systems today rely on attributes rather than projected decisions but I will make reference to both attribute and government decision models in this study.

Ratings systems generally are a summed total of a number of variables that are theorized to collectively reflect the level of risk to foreign investors. Although there is reasonably wide variance in the composition of the lists, there are some common components. These lists include 1) attributes of the government of the host country; 2) attributes of the social system; and 3) attributes of the international circumstances of the country. These attributes are considered to be the sources or possible causes of losses to investors.

A widely used example of such source categorizations is the ICRG. This model includes the following variables and weights:

> *ICRG Political Risk Components*
> ❑ Government Attributes
> - Government Stability 12 pts
> - Investment Profile 12 pts
> - Democratic Accountability 6 pts
> - Law and Order 6 pts
> - Military in politics 6 pts
> - Religion in Politics 6 pts
> - Bureaucracy Quality 4 pts
> ❑ Societal Attributes
> - Internal Conflict 12 pts
> - Corruption 6 pts
> - Ethnic Tensions 6 pts
> - Socioeconomic Conditions 12 pts
> ❑ International Environment
> - External Conflict 12 pts

Each variable has a weight that reflects its relative importance in the configuration of attributes that contribute to risk. For the published ratings, these are fixed for all investors. The maximum total number of political risk points is 100. The Actual Risk Points (ARP) achieved are interpreted on the following scale:[1]

Very High Risk	00.0 to 49.9 percent
High Risk	50.0 to 59.9 percent
Moderate Risk	60.0 to 69.9 percent
Low Risk	70.0 to 79.9 percent
Very Low Risk	80.0 to 100 percent

But this is just general advice. It gives a general idea of the magnitude of risk and possible problems in the investment environment. But what about management advice? There is really none of that here.

Similar methods exist for a number of models. Among these are BERI, S.J. Rundt & Associates, and the 1986 *Economist* model. The main categories are the same and many of the variables are similar, with some relatively minor variations.[2]

The PRS decision model also contains twelve variables. Several of these can be considered to be attributes, especially "Political Turmoil," which would fall into the 'attributes of the social system' category. The others are all deemed to be the results of direct or indirect government decisions. The model never uses all the variables in a single risk application but instead variables are used selectively in three areas of investment: 1) Financial transfers; 2) Direct investment; and 3) Exports. For each a letter grade is provided that parallels the usual evaluation system with 'A' at the top and 'D' at the bottom. The full set of variables provided is:

---

[1] "The International Country Risk Guide (ICRG) Rating System," in Llewellyn D. Howell, ed., *The Handbook of Country and Political Risk Analysis, 2nd Edition*, East Syracuse, NY: The PRS Group, 1998, p. 188.

[2] See Chapter 1 of this text for more explicit comparisons.

PRS Political Risk Components
- ❑ Societal Attributes
  - Political Turmoil
- ❑ Government Policies Related to:
  - Limitations on Equity
  - Operations Restrictions and Interference
  - Taxation Discrimination
  - Repatriation Restrictions
  - Exchange Inhibitions or Controls
  - Tariff Discrimination
  - Non-tariff Barrier Discrimination
  - Payment Delays
  - Fiscal and Monetary Expansion
  - Labor Cost Fluctuation
  - Foreign Debt Magnitude

I will refer to management tools below that relate to government decisions as distinct from government or societal attributes. However, these decisions may also be looked at as acts generating losses that are a function of attributes such as those listed for ICRG. For example, the ICRG attribute 'poor *bureaucracy quality*' may be the cause of the PRS government decision '*payment delays.*' Although bureaucracy quality is probably not the only cause of payment delays, it may be that, to some extent, a management response may be applied to both.

Political risk assessment is intended to assist foreign investors in managing their businesses located in foreign countries.[3] A country rating, such as a score of '74' from BERI or ICRG or a letter rating like 'B+' from PRS or 'BBB' from Standard and Poor's, is a statement about the country's overall risk. Overall risk is an indicator of many possible types of losses to the investing firm and will emanate from many sources. The types of losses can range from straightforward expropriation to subtle operations interference in a local assembly plant to civil strife damage from tribal warfare. Eight types of losses generated from political sources are discussed in Chapter 1.[4] I'll refer to these loss types below as *vul-*

---

[3] And by 'foreign investor' here I mean any investor not operating in its home cultural and/or political system. Since most political risk assessment systems provide ratings of developed as well as developing countries, a foreign investor here could be a Singaporean company investing in the U.S. or vice versa.

[4] Loss types have been categorized into eight categories: 1) Inconvertibility; 2) Expropriation; War damage; 4) Civil strife damage; 5) Contract repudiation; 6) Negative government actions; 7) Proc-

nerabilities. The sources can be as wide-ranging as ethnic or linguistic fraction-alization to extensive involvement of the military in political decision-making.

The point of identifying political risk probabilities with accurate assessments is to be able to avoid the costs of a probable loss or to manage the circumstances to reduce or even eliminate any damage. How does a country rating of '74' or 'B+' tell us about the source of the risk or about which management tool to apply? The answer, of course, is that it doesn't. The country rating can say "Don't go there!" (if it's a 'D') or it can say "Don't worry!" (if it's an 'A+'). For managing macro level concerns, the standardized country-level analyses can potentially be useful for the right circumstances. But relatively little actual risk today is at the macro level. This level of assessment was useful in the 1960s and 1970s when socialist or Communist governments were coming into power in the wake of the colonial era. Country-wide expropriations or control of currency were common and governments in the emerging states treated all foreign investors alike. We have passed that era.

In the 21st Century, selective and creeping expropriation is much more likely. Particular types of businesses are targeted by governments who pick out cash cows with little import-component dependency to exploit. International war has diminished greatly only to be replaced with an expansion of ethnic wars that are often contained in particular parts of the country. International politics and nationalistic attitudes sometimes enter the picture and even the nationalities, religions, and races of the investors become the basis of selective actions by governments or guerrilla groups.

So what if it's an in-between rating, like most are? What does a 'B' rating tell us about the chances of civil strife damage? About potential contract interference? About any of the specific dangers that foreign investors face? Obviously, very little. That is, the manager who is trying to figure out what to do in the way of dealing with risk, instead of just running from it, doesn't gain much from this unfocused assessment. If political risk is high, a foreign investor may choose to avoid the risk entirely by not investing or investing in a different national location. But this will also result in lost opportunity, and doesn't involve much in the way of management.

---

ess deterioration; and 8) Event intervention. See Llewellyn D. Howell, "Country and Political risk Analysis: Applications for Management," in L. D. Howell, ed., *The Handbook of Country and Political Risk Analysis, 3rd Edition*, East Syracuse, NY: The PRS Group, 2001, p. 2-3.

Narrow the Causal Problem Frame for the Industry, Firm, or Project

In addition to quantitative ratings, most political risk firms also provide qualitative assessments in the form of text. The text may provide more detail on specific problems in the country and narrow the sources of risk.[5] But this type of writing has to be general to address the many potential types of firms that may be investing. As noted above, PRS ratings are narrowed to three investment areas: financial transfers, foreign direct investment (manufacturing, mining, any investment with equity in the host country), and exports. Even this, however, is not enough.

If a financial firm has no facilities in the host country, it probably would incur little in the way of damaging consequences from the PRS variable Political Turmoil.[6] If, however, the firm has a branch or two in the capital city with physical property, then there might be more danger of damage and loss from riots, racial conflicts, or civil war. If it has 20 branches spread around the country, the danger would be much greater. The variable could be included or excluded from the rating calculation, depending on whether or not there were physical assets at risk. At minimum, the variable should be weighted according to the impact on the particular investor. It's clear that there is no 'one size fits all' for political risk assessments.

Charles Kennedy has noted managerial perceptions of risk from particular variables across a wide range of industries.[7] On a zero to three scale, managers in the pharmaceutical industry petroleum industry felt that political instability would have a great effect on them, rating it at 2.9. On the other hand, those in automobile exports scored instability only at 1.5. Other perceptions range widely in between. Both as a matter of perception and reality, risk varies according to industry, firm, and project.

---

[5] See, for example, any country study by PRS, which provides 30-40 pages of background, data, and commentary (examples may be found at http://www.prsgroup.com), and Bruce Gale's comments on political risk in Malaysia, at http://www.asiarisk.com/library2.html.

[6] The complete list of PRS variables is provided in "Political Risk Services," in Llewellyn D. Howell, ed., *The Handbook of Country and Political Risk Analysis, 3rd Edition*, East Syracuse, NY: The PRS Group, 2001.

[7] Charles R. Kennedy, Jr., *Political Risk Management*, New York: Quorum Books, 1987, pp. 68-69.

The consequence of this realization is that country ratings should be viewed not as the end product but rather as the medium by which individual variable ratings are provided to the end user. That is, the most valuable component of a

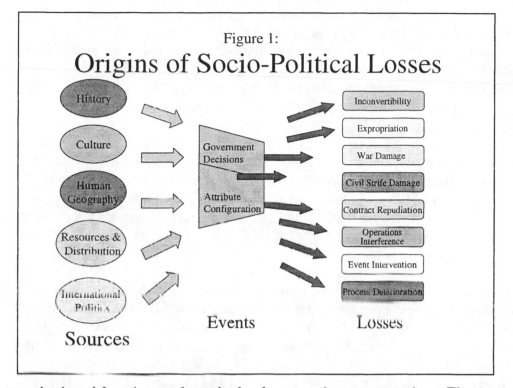

Figure 1:
Origins of Socio-Political Losses

quantitative risk rating package is the data, not the country rating. The user can then develop a rating to fit its own needs. How does this process work?

What is necessary is that each individual investor look first at its *own* vulnerabilities for *any* foreign investment situation. These may be drawn from the eight categories suggested or drawn more narrowly. Then once these are identified, work backward to identify the sources of the particular risk (see Figure 1).

The investor needs to begin by identifying its particular vulnerabilities in the foreign environment. What types of losses might occur for this industry, firm, or project? Then what are the sources of those losses. This next stage has to be a causal analysis. Given the context and practice of foreign investment, this doesn't have to a formal mathematical analysis, but rather should be a sit-down session with knowledgeable managers and consultants, including both those familiar with the firm and its operations and those who know the host country well. This can always be a situation where company managers undertake the entire analysis with the help of published text country assessments but there is always much missing in any written study. These are also written for a general audience.

Here's an example of how this would work. If we are talking about a mining company, it is likely that 1) a contract with the government is entailed; 2) a large number of local employees will be hired; 3) ore will be shipped from a host country port facility; 4) the facility will be located in a remote and rural area of the country; and 5) there is considerable equity in buildings, general infrastructure, and equipment. There are always more elements to the situation than this but these will serve to illustrate the problem and the process.

If there is a government contract, the vulnerability is to *contract repudiation.* The investor needs to know, first, what situational characteristics or attribute types have historically led to abrogation or disputes over terms of contracts. It then needs to know if any of those characteristics are present in the host country government. And it is important to understand that repudiation or interference can occur at many levels, specifically national, provincial, city, village, or even tribal.

If there are a large number of employees, the company's human resource office will have to deal with intercultural sensibilities among the employees, cross-cultural sensitivity between the employer and the employees, government determined hiring policies, affirmative action requirements, and gender parity problems related to the particular society. The firm's employee base will invite a variety of types of both *negative government actions* and *negative events* such as politically motivated strikes.

If a port facility is required, the firm will be vulnerable to any action affecting that port or the exporting ability of the host country. *Sanctions and blockades* in diplomatic controversies could be one problem but so would acts of war or sabotage conducted by another country, including the home country. *War damage* is not common but remains a central category of political risk insurance coverage for a reason.

If the firm is operating in a remote area of the country, it could be vulnerable to *civil strife damage.* There is a vulnerability on two counts. The first is that conflicts between ethnic groups or between guerrilla groups and the government usually arise and are fostered in remote areas. The second is that host government forces are usually arrayed in urban areas and around the seat of government. It takes them longer to get to confrontations in the more remote areas, if they ever get there. In the meantime, otherwise preventable damage could be done.

Any firm with equity is vulnerable to *expropriation*. In today's world, that includes many forms of "creeping" expropriation, as well as nationalizations and seizures. And, of course, expropriation can occur at all the same levels as contract repudiation, from national to tribal.

There are more vulnerabilities than these for this firm but these provide examples to work with and illustrate the process of initial identification of possible problems for a firm no matter where it is located. Some of these vulnerabilities can be responded to directly or have to be. Others can be dealt with at their sources. The next step is to determine if the conditions that lead to exploitation of these vulnerabilities are present in the host country, and in the region of that country where the project is located.

Causal Bases for Vulnerabilities

Let's follow up on two examples of the vulnerabilities and hypothesize a bit about how losses in these categories might arise. The two examples are civil strife damage and expropriation. Expropriation is the most notorious of losses, dating especially to the anti-colonial period of the 1960s and 1970s. Civil strife damage was the most common political risk insurance claim paid by OPIC in the 1990s.

For Civil Strife Damage, the example of Freeport McMoRan in Indonesia is instructive. In 1996, Freeport was struck by rioting at its copper mine in Irian Jaya, the eastern-most island of Indonesia. Buildings were damaged, with windows broken and other damage occurred as well: mining and personal use vehicles were hit, and production was halted for three days.[8] Underlying the complaints of the rioters were several familiar situational attributes found in political risk models. These included 1) Ethnic Tension (ICRG, *Economist*, BERI); 2) Political Fractionalization (BERI); 3) Religion in Politics (ICRG, *Economist*); and Poor Socioeconomic Conditions (ICRG).

The region around the Irian Jaya mine is populated by tribal peoples who are a distinct racial group from the Indonesian leadership in Java and from Indonesians generally in the rest of the country. Moreover, these people are also subdivided among themselves into tribes with different cultures and agendas. The latter ac-

---

[8]"Irian Jaya mine resumes work," *Financial Times*, March 15, 1996.

count for one element of political fractionalization. Another arises from within Indonesia itself, where the political culture of Jakarta, thousands of miles away, fails to reach into many of the hundreds of populated islands that compose the country. Many employees and villagers in the area surrounding the mine look to Freeport McMoRan as the local government. That in turn, increases the concern and intervention of the national government in Jakarta that wants both to continue to receive the income from the mine and maintain its political control. Add to the picture the fact that most Indonesians are Muslim (about 95%) while the Irian Jaya population is mostly Christian and other local religions. In socioeconomic terms, the area has been neglected by the Indonesian government and is among the poorest in a very poor country.

The melange of racial, religious, cultural, political, and economic disparities make a volatile mix, already resulting in several major losses to Freeport McMo-Ran. More importantly for our purposes, it's a useful illustration of societal attributes and vulnerability to "civil strife damage." These sources of strife were evident to any trained eye well before the initiation of work at the mine. The question is 'were the responses of managers prepared in advance for these likely events?'

What about expropriation? Without going into as much detail as in the example above, acts of expropriation can also be seen in attributes and projected decisions of national or local governments. 1) Authoritarian (*Economist*, ICRG, BERI) institutions are more likely to have the opportunity and leverage to expropriate. 2) When the military is heavily involved in politics (ICRG, *Economist*), legal principles are more likely to be ignored. 3) Unstable political leadership (ICRG) often finds it necessary to take drastic actions to justify its existence, especially new governments coming to power with a widely variant political philosophy from the previous government. 4) When radical--and especially leftist--forces take over a government (BERI) both ideology and a sense of nationalist ownership create an environment in which seizures and expropriation become more likely. And 5) a weak legal system (ICRG) often leaves little or no recourse in the courts for a foreign investor to obtain a return of equity seized by a government at any level.

As was suggested above in noting the two model types--attributes and decisions--management response to risk can occur at either or both of the levels described. In the first example, there are responses to both the underlying causes (e.g. ethnic tension) and the social outcome (e.g. civil strife damage). For the second, management principles may be applied in dealing with a weak legal system (for example, externally guaranteed contracts) and with expropriation itself (expropriation insurance). Some tools are multiple-use tools; others are specific to the task.

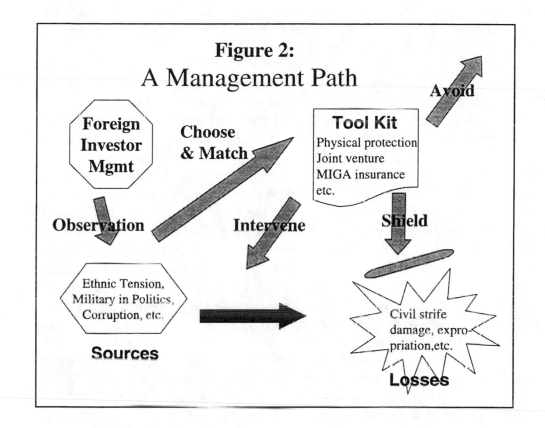

Figure 2:
A Management Path

The Management Tool Kit

For companies that pay attention to political risk, there are five possible general responses that a firm can take. To make some distinction between these broader responses and more specific actions that can be taken by investment managers, I will refer to the broad responses as 'Level I' tools and to the more specific as 'Level II.' While all five of the Level I responses are decisions that company or investment managers make—and all therefore can be referred to as 'management'—each entails a different strategic approach to handling the effort to prevent losses arising from socio-political risk. The general process of political risk assessment and then ensuing risk management is described in Figure 2.

Level I Management Tools

The first is **avoidance**. If a firm finds that it has no ability to deal with a particular risk or a set of risks in a country, it can make a decision either to *not invest abroad at all* or *to shift its investment interests to another country or location with less risk.* Both of these options are common, with the former more common than the latter, at least until the era of globalization.

The second is **deterrence**. In this process, the investing firm can act to prevent particular problems from arising. It is now recognized that political risk insurance can sometimes play a role as a deterrent. This can be referred to as "impact" political risk insurance, as distinct from "compensation" political risk insurance. These are discussed further below. If a firm is known to have political risk insurance from the Overseas Private Investment Corporation (OPIC), for example, a government might be less likely to expropriate assets of that firm because it knows that OPIC-insured properties become the possession of the U.S. government if it pays the insurance claim.[9] Insurance from the Multilateral Investment Guarantee Agency (MIGA) of the World Bank has the same effect, also including possible consequences affecting lending from the World Bank and its affiliates. This approach can have its own dangers. Historically, many firms have deterred government interference by creating an alliance with the government in power. Since the government has a stake in business development, it is less likely to dispute its own source of profits. But if the government has a dramatic loss of support or is ousted in a coup or rebellion, that same firm can suddenly find itself on the side of the new government's enemy.

The third is **process management**. It is in this category that most options occur. Here management recognizes a source of danger and intervenes to prevent it from reaching its culminating effects. For example, if a mining firm is aware of local ethnic rivalries that could result in violence in the workplace, the firms managers can exercise discretion in placement of supervisors, in numbers of particular ethnic group employees hired, and in an appropriate balance in training, advancement, and awards.

---

[9] OPIC is an agency of the U.S. government that offers political risk insurance to qualified American companies investing abroad. For a brief description of OPIC and a case where the U.S. government pursued a government after it had expropriated two power plants, see Llewellyn D. Howell, "The Overseas Private Investment Corporation (OPIC): An Application of Risk Management—MidAmerican Energy in Indonesia," in L. D. Howell, ed., *The Handbook of Country and Political Risk Analysis, 3rd Edition*, East Syracuse, NY: The PRS Group, 2001.

The fourth is **compensation protection**, otherwise known as *political risk insurance*. For the most part, political risk management means making decisions that keep the firm or business from harm. Political risk insurance has its primary use in dealing with the aftermath of damage, reducing it rather than preventing it. Since political risk insurance usually involves a deductible and often payments are a result of negotiation rather than set amounts, this does not amount to full recovery of losses. The deductible may be 10% and thus still amounts to a considerable loss to the firm. In addition, peripheral damage often occurs that is not or cannot be covered by insurance. For example, Keene Industries in Liberia suffered a number of losses in the early 1990s in Liberia when attacked on several occasions by elements of an ongoing rebellion in that country.[10] Keene was partially compensated for losses of vehicles, food stores, equipment, and some product but received no compensation on lost production, evacuation costs for expatriate personnel, or wages to employees who had to be paid despite a lack of actual work. Note that *compensation political risk insurance* should be distinguished from *impact political risk insurance* as being from two different categories of response.

Fifth is a risk **offset**. In this instance a loss is balanced in a larger picture by reducing overall risk by making "a substantial part of [the firm's] profits in another part of the value-added chain or in related operations."[11]

Level II Management Tools

In today's context of high information, knowing the risk and its nature should be able to put investors in a position of being able to counter the risk with management actions that alleviate the level of risk. Referred to as *process management* above, there are many options for managers who seek to head off or resolve socio-political threats to their firms. Here is a set of possibilities that can be regarded as a "tool kit" for managers and investment decision-makers. The vulnerabilities (loss categories) to which the management tool might apply are underlined:

---

[10] One of these instances is examined in Llewellyn D. Howell, "Keene Industries in Liberia: A Political Risk Case Study and Teaching Note," in *International Studies Notes*, Vol. 23, No. 2 (Spring 1998), pp. 18-28.

[11] Lewis T. Wells, Jr., "God and Fair Competition: Does the Foreign Direct Investor Face Still Other Risks in Emerging Markets?" in Theodore H. Moran, ed., *Managing International Political Risk*, Malden, MA: Blackwell Publishers, 1998, p. 33.

Get Expertise for Identifying Risk

The foreign investor needs two kinds of expertise. The first is expertise on the firm in order to determine vulnerabilities. This kind of expertise usually has to come from within the firm, although outside consultants familiar with the industry can help. The second is expertise on the host country. This almost always has to come from outside the firm. One of the biggest mistakes an investing firm can make is to send the company's VP to the capital city of the host country, to stay in a five-star hotel and meet with host country nationals who speak the language of the investor. True country experts are necessary to give a full and unbiased picture of the business environment. They can get beyond the English language news sources and have a "feel" for the country that investors ordinarily don't have. <u>Country expertise is needed no matter what the form of political risk or potential loss</u>.

Purchase Impact Political Risk Insurance

By "impact" political risk insurance I mean insurance that has an impact on the government of the country prior to any political acts that might compromise the investor. This is especially important for situations of <u>potential expropriation</u>, <u>limits on currency conversion</u>, <u>government interference with operations</u>, or <u>contract repudiation</u>. Impact insurance is that which plays a role in *preventing* negative government actions. For example, if an investor has OPIC insurance, the government will know that if the investor loses equity to them, the U.S. government will become the owner of the equity after payment of a claim and that the U.S. will come after compensation from the host government. After the Indonesian government expropriated Mid- American Energy's two power plants in 1998 and OPIC paid the claim in 1999, the U.S. actively discouraged other loans and assistance to the Indonesian government until the Indonesian government agreed to pay the $290 million lost by MidAmerican (and therefore by the U.S. government). OPIC and MIGA have guarantee agreements with host country governments. Importantly, they have the power to back them up.

Negotiate Better Profit Margins

Where the host country is a seller's market for foreign investors (and most are), conditions in the country that discourage such investment can be dealt with by asking the government to waive or alter limitations that would ordinarily be placed on the investor. For example, if ethnic divisions in the country are high, and if there is a limit on the percentage of profit that can be repatriated, then the investor might negotiate to take home a larger percentage as insurance against the possibility that the ethnic tension might result in conflict with damage to facilities. The investment, of course, has to have some advantage for the host government. This tool would be useful in any situations where there are the makings of domestic conflict that is beyond the direct control of the government and, ultimately, <u>civil strife damage</u>, <u>event intervention</u> (like kidnapping), or other acts generated by the society.

Obtain or Provide Physical Protection

Some of the larger investors have chosen to protect their facilities by hiring armed guards, purchase and use of armored cars, placing protective perimeters and other barriers, forming their own small armies, or 'hiring' components of the national army of the host country. This protection ranges from that against <u>kidnapping</u> to the guarding of oil pipelines against <u>civil strife</u> and <u>event intervention damage</u>. There is also considerable danger here, too, in that some protective forces get out of hand and some have been charged with human rights abuses, creating more risk than they inhibit.

Enter International Alliances (Wells)[12]

From a broad company perspective, one way to manage risk in one country is to spread it across countries. That is, one firm can open investments in several countries, some with lesser levels of risk, to help bear the burden if one has difficulty. More effective is to develop a consortium with other firms in the same industry to spread resources over a larger number of projects. This may be across countries or simply in different regions of the same country. Although this may increase the possibility of some loss, it can eliminate the probability of a large loss. International alliances are especially effective where the host government is likely to be involved in the potential loss, areas like <u>expropriation</u>, <u>inconvertibility</u>, and <u>contract repudiation</u>.

Share Investment with Other Firms

Joint venturing with other foreign firms in the same industry can spread any possible losses. Of course, profits are spread too. The tool

---

[12] See Wells, *op.cit.*, pp. 33-37 for further descriptions and examples.

is useful for those cases where the only recourse seems to be loss reduction, such as in <u>civil strife damage</u> or <u>war damage,</u> rather than for those instances where some intervention with the government might work.

Build Local Political Alliances

In order to head off problems in the local community that arise in response to the presence of the investor operation, it is necessary—at minimum—to be fully aware of the nature of the local political structure and know who the players are. Without taking sides in an explicit sense, cooperative relations with local governments and institutions (such as welfare agencies) is more than a matter of good public relations. By making itself known as a positive force in community development, the investor can head off <u>local government operations interference</u> and <u>contract abrogation</u>. The focus here is on relations between the investor and government processes.

Build Community Indebtedness

Just as the investor can deal from the start with government institutions to head off misunderstandings and eliminate distance between them, the investor can likewise direct efforts at building a relationship with the social community itself. Allies can be created in the population to deter effects of xenophobia and mistrust, thereby heading off acts of <u>[event] intervention</u> that occur between the community and outsiders. Singapore companies operating in the Indonesian islands of the Riau group, for example, have taken such steps as providing scholarships to local high school students, in an area where funding for high school tuition and books (and even clothing) can make a difference in educational accomplishments and local development.

Apply knowledgeable human resource management

Every community in which an investor operates has its divisions. The investor cannot be seen to be taking sides, and yet many do so unknowingly. In many Southeast Asian countries there are local Chinese communities that provide a pool of educated and skilled personnel, often experienced in business, management, and technology at a level beyond that of other ethnic groups. On a purely skill basis, it always tempting to hire proportionally larger numbers from this group. But the investor has to be concerned about relations among employees of different racial, religious, linguistic, and cultural backgrounds, especially including those between supervisors and other workers. Local resentments can pour into the workplace and disturb and disrupt production. This form of <u>event intervention</u> can not only limit production but can explode into larger acts of <u>civil strife,</u> all stemming from disputes over opportunity distribution. Attention has to be given to all forms of fragmentation in the local community: race, religion, language, gender, social standing, tribal affiliation, caste, even physical size. HR personnel need to be extremely knowledgeable about the local culture to be able to prevent problems that can easily arise in environments where the investor is a newcomer. And this particular intervention of good management has to occur at the earliest possible stage of the investment. Mistakes made early on often set the tone and cannot be overcome later.

Make Money in Related Operations (Wells)

Where there is a value-added chain for an investor, that chain can be segmented in terms of political risk. The investor can then focus on making profits in the less risky segments of the chain. Wells uses the example of Enron in India, which could have chosen to make its profits in the supply of fuel to its Maharashtra power generation plant rather than from operation of the power plant itself. "If the core project is squeezed, peripheral activities may assure adequate returns." (p. 33) This can be a useful technique for management of risks of <u>expropriation</u> and <u>operations interference</u>.

Joint Venture with a Local Partner

Sometimes a JV with a local partner can reduce the impact of some risk, especially where the foreign investors may be the target of <u>nationalism</u> or <u>xenophobia,</u> and thereby of <u>civil strife damage</u> or <u>event intervention</u>. Great care must be taken, however, in the choice of the partner. A partner from the wrong side in local disputes may make the investor a target when it might not otherwise be.

Avoid Blame Associated with Privatization (Wells)

Privatization often entails price increases for the product of the industry taken out of government assets or ownership. If an investor buys in at an early stage, blame is likely to be directed at the foreigner. Investors can anticipate this and require that any price increases take place before it takes over. This tool is useful in circumstances of potential <u>civil strife damage</u> or <u>local government negative actions</u> that might be in response to societal conditions or concerns.

Prepare for Regulation (Wells)

Particularly at a point of new or recent privatization, few or no regulations will have been established. Anticipating the possibility that the firm might be out of step with future regulations, exemptions can be sought or the government can be asked to establish private sector regulations before funds are committed. Managing this problem will help fend off <u>contract disputes</u>, <u>negative government actions</u> (national and local), and <u>event intervention</u> in the society where the investor must operate.

Involve Strong International Interests (Wells)

Like with impact political risk insurance, if influential partners are involved in a project there is less likelihood of some forms of negative government actions. This is particularly so if projects are funded by institutions such as the Asian Development Bank or the IMF. International organizations also may have an effect but these seem to be declining in importance in recent years. (Wells, p. 35) Negative actions such as <u>expropriation</u>, declarations of <u>inconvertibility</u>, <u>limitations on remittances</u>, or <u>contract repudiation</u> can be inhibited via the power of the international partner, especially when it is a lending institution from which the host government would hope to get further funding. When risk is high, it might be worthwhile seeking out a particular lender to get this kind of protection.

Seek Sensible Methods of Dispute Settlement (Wells)

In a globalized system, it is no longer a sign of lack of trust to seek international arbitration or to build mechanisms for such adjudication into initial contracts. This tool is most effective for larger investments but sometimes can be utilized for smaller ones if negotiations are handled carefully. It can be applied where there is a concern about possible <u>operations interference</u>, <u>contract repudiation</u>, or <u>expropriation</u>.

Design Financial Structure to Minimize Risk (Wells)

"The record for honoring debt from parents and other affiliates seems almost as strong as that of debt from independent financial institutions. As a result, a financial structure that depends heavily on debt may provide more security than one with a lower debt/equity ratio." (Wells, pp. 34-35) This tool will be useful if there is a vulnerability to <u>expropriation</u>, <u>negative government actions</u>, or <u>contract frustration</u>.

Choose Defensible Process for Negotiating Entry (Wells)

Transparency is increasingly expected in the world of the WTO and globalization. Unfortunately, the level of secrecy remains high in the competitive world of multinational and international business. Companies still too often think in terms of getting a special deal or "engage in bargaining processes that are not competitive." (Wells, p. 36) In the darkness of some of these negotiations, illegalities, favoritism, and unreasonable terms often characterize the outcome. Investors can avoid <u>negative government actions</u> later by keeping the deal open and clean from the beginning. If effect, the investment manager should plan from the beginning how he will be able to navigate both the judicial system of the host country and the court of public opinion.

Look for Innovative Forms of Agreement (Wells)

In sensitive areas of investment, such as those dealing with natural resources, monopolies, and basic services, it is sometimes useful to separate ownership from control and earnings. The investment can be structured such that nominal ownership is in the hands of host country nationals while major decisions and sufficient earnings are kept in the hands of the foreign investor. This tight structuring obviously has to be done at the front end of the investment. In the long run it can protect against <u>civil strife</u> directed at the firm and from both <u>national and local operations interference.</u> Building change into an agreement anticipates the need for contracts to evolve and heads off a perceived need by the government to <u>alter or repudiate contracts</u>. 'Build, operate, and transfer' (BOT) arrangements are one form of anticipating the problem of staleness of contracts.

The Slippery Slope of Bribery

No realistic discussion of political risk management is complete without some discussion of the role of bribery and other forms of corruption and favoritism. It has to be recognized that payoffs to prevent problems (strikes, sabotage, delays, unwanted regulations, etc.) are sought widely, in both emerging and developed markets. And, of course, the use of these techniques can provide some short-term solutions. But more than any other tool that is at the hand of the foreign investor, corruptive acts lay the groundwork for far more problems than they resolve. Not the least of these is product deterioration. Hiring the relatives of an influential local official can, for example, mean that the most skilled managers or workers are *not* employed. Corruption can often lead to production shortcuts to make up the cost of money lost in process. Favoritism is always recognized in local communities and is seen as side taking, leading to the possibility of cleavages that can be more of a problem than anything that was resolved. Most importantly, even in most places where corruption is common, it is also illegal. This is particularly a threat for American companies where it is also illegal in the U.S. as well as in the local context. This is a tool that is available but is clearly a double-edged sword and is best left in the toolkit.

The Manager's Responsibility: Picking the Right Tool

This list is only partial. It represents an effort to link management tools with vulnerabilities and to make the manager aware of the fact that there *are* tools available for dealing with political risk. But vulnerabilities still need to be linked with country or regional attributes and government decision proclivities in order to determine whether the recommended tools should be applied. The investor will have vulnerabilities no matter where it chooses to invest. The key question is 'can the vulnerabilities be exploited in the chosen investment country (or sub-region)?' Here is the management task then: 1) match the investment and the firm with *vulnerabilities* (for example)...

> *Expropriation*
> *Contract Repudiation*
> ***Civil Strife Damage***
> *Event Intervention*
> *et al.*

...then 2) match vulnerabilities with *sources of risk*...
For example, for Event intervention (Kidnapping of managers and workers), the sources might be:

> ***Ethnic tension***
> *Military power abuses*
> *Religion in politics*
> *Xenophobia*

...then match the exploitable vulnerabilities and their causal sources to tools:
For **ethnic tension**,
Build local political alliances

Build community indebtedness
Include physical protection
Develop alliances
Purchase compensation political risk insurance[13]

Several tasks are therefore laid out for the managers of a foreign invest-ment in dealing with political risk. First, they have to know the investment cli-mate well, but they also must know their own firm and operations well in order to determine vulnerabilities. This may seem obvious and in many cases is. But it is still often the case that investors get caught off guard by unfolding events in emerging markets and end up with significant losses. We only need to check the claims lists at the companies providing political risk insurance.

Managers have to be able to investigate the local sources of loss outcomes. That is, someone in the firm or someone hired by the firm has to be able to dissect Indonesia but also Irian Jaya if that is where the firm is going to be located. That dissection involves both societal and governmental processes, including at the lo-cal level.

Finally, a political risk manager has to have a *toolkit* available from Day One. There is an array of tools, at two levels, that a manager can apply to specific problems generated by the society and political system in which they must oper-ate. The manager must know specifically what those tools are and what they can do, but most importantly, the manager has to know that *there is a toolkit*. Use of those tools is necessary at the earliest stages of a foreign investment and must be a part of the plan from the beginning. Political risk insurance is a good reminder. Insurance can only be purchased before the business or project is started. It can't be purchased after the project is underway and it is suddenly discovered that it is located in the middle of a hornet's nest. At the same point the manager is making a decision about political risk insurance, he must also make at least preliminary decisions about which management tools he will apply. In emerging markets, he certainly will need to employ some. And as with any other aspect of good busi-ness practice, planning ahead is the key for dealing successfully with political risk. The tools are there. All we have to do is know enough to use them.

---

[13] ...since *impact* political risk insurance is not going to stop ethnic warfare. It is also important to know which form of political risk insurance to contract for. In this case 'civil strife' or 'political violence' damage insurance would be needed, as distinct from inconvertibility, expropriation, war damage, or contract repudiation insurance.

SELECTED REFERENCES

Bernstein, Peter, *Against The Gods: The Remarkable Story of Risk*, NY: John Wiley & Sons, Inc., 1998.

"Countries in Trouble: who's on the skids?" *The Economist*, Vol. 301, December 20, 1986, pp. 69-72.

Hodgetts, Richard M. and Fred Luthans, *International Management*, New York: McGraw-Hill, Inc., 1991, pp. 118-119.

Howell, Llewellyn D., "Country and Political Risk Analysis: Foundations for Foreign Direct Investment," in L. D. Howell, ed., *The Handbook of Country and Political Risk Analysis*, 2nd Edition, East Syracuse, NY: The PRS Group, 1998, pp. 3-11.

_____, "Operationalizing Political Risk in International Business: The Concept of a Politically-based Loss," in Jerry Rogers, ed., *Global Risk Assessments Book 4*, Riverside, CA: GRA Inc., 1997.

_____, "Political Risk and Political Loss for Foreign Investment", *The International Executive*, Vol. 34 No. 6, November-December 1992, pp. 485-498.

"The International Country Risk Guide (ICRG) Rating System," in Llewellyn D. Howell, ed., *The Handbook of Country and Political Risk Analysis, 2nd Edition*, East Syracuse, NY: The PRS Group, 1998.

Kennedy, Charles R. Jr., *Political Risk Management*, New York: Quorum Books, 1987.

Monti-Belkaoui, Janice and Ahmed Riahi-Bekaoui, *The Nature, Estimation, and Management of Political Risk*, Westport, CN: Quorum Books, 1998.

Moran, Theodore H., ed., *Managing International Political Risk*, Malden, MA: Blackwell Publishers, 1998 (A).

Moran, Theodore H., *Foreign Direct Investment and Development*, Washington, DC: Institute for International Economics, 1998 (B).

OPIC, "Insurance Claims Experience to Date", September 30, 2000.

"Political Risk Services," in Llewellyn D. Howell, ed., *The Handbook of Country and Political Risk Analysis, 3rd Edition*, East Syracuse, NY: The PRS Group, 2001.

Wells, Louis T., Jr., "God and Fair Competition: Does the Foreign Direct Investor Face Still Other Risks in Emerging Markets?" in Theodore H. Moran, ed., *Managing International Political Risk*, Malden, MA: Blackwell Publishers, 1998, pp. 15-43.

A Selected Article Bibliography
Llewellyn D. Howell, Susana G. Howell, Toni Siragusa

Akhter, Humayun and Robert F. Lusch, (1987),"Political Risk: A Structural Analysis," *Advances*.

Al-Tabtabai, Hashem and Alex P. Alex, (2000),"Modeling the Cost of Political Risk in International Construction Projects," *Project Management Journal*, September.

Alon, Ilan and Matthew A. Martin, (1998),"A Normative Model of Macro Political Risk Assessment," *Multinational Business Review*, Fall.

Anderson, Kim, "The Political Risk Squeeze," (1991), *Global Finance,* December.

Andrew, Craig B., (1991), "Reflections on the Career Evolution of a Business Risk Analyst," *Risk Management Review*, Fall.

Arnott, Robert D. and Roy D. Henriksson, (1989),"A Disciplined Approach to Global Asset Allocation," *Financial Analysts Journal*, March/April.

Austin, James E., "Country Analysis Framework," (1989), *Harvard Business Review*, December.

Avasthi, David D., (1992), "As the Walls Crumble, Upheavals Spur Demand for Political Risk Coverage," *Business Insurance*, July.

Ayali, Noam, (2000),"Insuring Political Risk in the Emerging Markets," *International Finance Law Review,* January.

Bailey, Kathleen C., (1983), "Profiling an Effective Political Risk Assessment Team," *Risk Management*, February.

Baker, James C. and M. Anaam Hashmi, (1988), "Political Risk Management: Steering Clear of Risky Business," *Risk Management*, October.

Baliga, B. R., (1984), "World-Views and Multinational Corporations Investments in the Less Developed Countries," *The Columbia Journal of World Business*, Summer.

Banker, Pravin, (1983),"You're the Best Judge of Foreign Risks," *Harvard Business Review*, March/April.

Barovick, Richard,(1997), "Zurich Jumps into The Political Risk Insurance Arena: OPIC Official At Helm of Subsidiary Effort," *Journal of Commerce,* May.

Beaty, David and Oren Harari, (1987),"Divestment and Disinvestment from South Africa: A Reappraisal," *California Management Review*, Summer.

Bird, Graham, (1986)"New Approaches to Country Risk," *Lloyds Bank Review*, October.

Boddewyn, Jean J. and Thomas L. Brewer, (1994) "International-Business Political Behavior: New Theoretical Directions," *Academy of Management Review*, No. 1.

Bowman, Robert L., (1995), "Are You Covered?" *World Trade,* March.

Bradley, David G., (1977),"Managing Against Expropriation," *Harvard Business Review*, July/August.

Brandman, James, (1999),"Terrorism, Fanaticism, Extremism: On the Rise," *Global Finance,* June.

Brewer, Thomas L., (1991),"Country Risk and Country Instability: The Case of Turkey," *Global Finance Journal,* Vol. 2.

_____, (1983), "The Instability of Governments and the Instability of Controls on Funds Transfers by Multinational Enterprises: Implications for Political Risk Analysis,", *Journal of International Business Studies*, Winter.

_____, (1981), "Political Risk Assessment for Foreign Direct Investment Decisions," *Columbia Journal of World Business,* Spring.

_____, (1983), "Political Sources of Risk in the International Money Markets: Conceptual, Methodological, and Interpretive Refinements," *Journal of International Business Studies*, Spring/Summer.

Broadfoot, Robert, "The Importance of Political Risk," (1998), *Political and Economic Risk Consultancy, Ltd. Library*, October.

Bromhead, Laurence, "A Slightly Riskier Place," (1989), *Euromoney: The Journal of the World's Capital and Money Markets*, Summer.

Burstein, Daniel, "The Risk Analysts Survive a Shakeout," (1983), *International Management*, October.

Burson, Harold, "Damage Control in a Crisis," (1985), *Management Review,* December.

Burton, F. N. and Hisashi Inoue, (1987), "A Country Risk Appraisal Model of Foreign Asset Expropriation in Developing Countries," *Applied Economics*, August.

Butler, Kirt C., and Domingo Castelo Joaquin, (1998), "A Note on Political Risk and the Required Return on Foreign Direct Investment," *Journal of International Business Studies* Vol. 29.

Chase, C.D. et. al., (1988), "The Relevance of Political Risk in Direct Foreign Investment," *Management International Review,* Vol. 28.

Citron, Joel-Thomas and Gerald Nickelsburg, (1987), "Country Risk and Political Instability," *Journal of Development Economics*, Vol. 25.

Clark, Ephraim, (1997), "Valuing Political Risk," *Journal of International Money and Finance*, Vol. 16.

Coady, E. Patrick, (1992), "Global Change and the World Bank," *The Bankers Magazine*, May/June.

Collins, J. Markham, and William S. Sekely, (1988), "Cultural Influences on International Capital Structure," *Journal of International Business Studies*, Spring.

Cook, Thomas A., (1989)"Political Risk: Not for the Fainthearted," *Best's Review*, February.

Coplin, William D., and Michael K. O'Leary, (1992), "1992-97 World Political Risk Forecast," *Planning Review*, March/April.

_____, (1985), "The 1985 Political Climate for International Business: a Forecast of Risk in 82 Countries," *Planning Review*, May.

_____, (1995),"On the Threshold of the 21st Century: A Surprising Wealth of Business Opportunities," *Planning Review,* March/April.

_____, (1983), "Systematic Political Risk Analysis for Planners," *Planning Review*, January.

Cosset, Jean-Claude, and Jean-Marc Suret, (1995), "Political Risk and the Benefits of International Portfolio Diversification," *Journal of International Business Studies,* Vol. 26.

Covaleski, John M., (1993), "After the Bloodshed, Russia Holds Promise," *Best's Review*, December.

Daniel, Druckman, and Justin Green, (1984), "Is Marcos Vulnerable? Analysis of Regime Stability in the Philippines," *Planning Review*, Vol. 12.

Dewitt, Peter R., and Jeff Madura, (1986), "How Banks Assess Country Risk," *World of Banking: The International Magazine of Bank Management*, January/February.

Diamonte, Robin, John M. Liew and Ross L. Stevens, (1996), "Political Risk in Emerging and Developed Markets," *Financial Analysts Journal*, May/June.

Dichtl, Erwin and H.G. Koglmayr, (1986). "Country Risk Ratings," *Management International Review*, Vol. 26.

Dooley, Michael P. and Peter Isard,(1980), "Capital Controls, Political Risk, and Deviation from Interest Rate Parity," *Journal of Political Economy*, April.

Droker, Linda and Jeffrey Hardee, (1983), "Dialogue Focuses Attention on ASEAN Markets," *Business America*, November.

Druckman, Daniel and Justin Green, (1984), "Is Marcos Vulnerable? Analysis of Regime Stability in the Philippines," *Planning Review*, November.

Dugan, William E., (1999), "Global Dangers: Political Risk Part I," *Risk Management*, September.

Easton, William R., (1998), "Risk Mitigation and Trade Finance: How to Analyze the Export Transaction," *Commercial Lending Review,* Fall.

Erb, Claude B., Harvey Campbell, and Tadas E. Viskanta, (2000), "Political Risk, Economic Risk and Financial Risk," *Financial Analysts Journal,* Summer.

Fairlamb, David and Henriette Sender, (1983), "How Good Are Country Risk Forecasters?" *Dun's Business Month*, May.

Fagre, Nathan and Louis T. Wells, (1982), "Bargaining Power of Multinationals and Host Governments," *Journal of International Business Studies*, Fall.

Fatehi, Kamal, (1994), "Capital Flight from Latin America as a Barometer of Political Instability," *Journal of Business Research*, July.

_____, (1994), "The Effect of Sociopolitical Instability on the Flow of Different Types of Foreign Direct Investment," *Journal of Business Research,* September.

Kamal Fatehi. and M.Hossein Safizadeh, (1989), "The Association Between Political Instability and Flow of Foreign Direct Investment," *Management International Review,* Vol. 29.

Feils, Dorothee J. and Florin M. Sabac, (2000), "The Impact of Political Risk on the Foreign Direct Investment Decision: A Capital Budgeting Analysis," *Engineering Economist*, Vol. 45.

Ferguson, Bryce, (2000), "A Consistent, Global Approach to Risk," *Journal of Lending & Credit Risk Management,* February.

Fisher, Brian, (1999), "Risk in Managing Emerging Market External Debt Portfolios," *Emerging Markets Quarterly,* Winter.

Fitzpatrick, Mark, (1983), "The Definition and Assessment of Political Risk in International Business: A Review of the Literature," *Academy of Management Review*, Vol. 8.

Flint, Perry, (1990), "A Risk Worth Taking: Political Risk Insurance is a Sensitive Subject Among Airlines," *Air Transport World*, August.

Friedmann, Roberto, and Jonghoon Kim, (1988), "Political Risk and International Marketing," *The Columbia Journal of World Business,* Winter.

Frynas, Jedrzej George, (1998), "Political Instability and Business: Focus on Shell in Nigeria," *Third World Quarterly*, Vol. 19.

Garten, Jeffrey, (1997), "Troubles Ahead in Emerging Markets," *Harvard Business Review,* May/June.

_____, (1998), "Opening Doors for Business in China," *Harvard Business Review*, May/June.

Gentile, Gary, (1998), "Can Political Risk Be Quantified? - While Measuring Beta Is a Science, Measuring Political Risk Is Most Certainly an Elusive Art," *Financial Planning*, September.

Ghadar, Fariborz, (1982), "Political Risk and the Erosion of Control: the Case of the Oil Industry," *Columbia Journal of World Business*, Fall.

Gillespie, K., (1989), "Political Risk Implications for Exporters, Contractors and Foreign Licensors: the Iranian Experience," *Management International Review*, Vol. 29.

Glasse, James, (1990), "Foreign Business in China Responds to Political Instability," *Multinational Business,* Summer.

Goldsmith, Arthur, (1994), "Political Freedom and the Business Climate: Outlook for Development in Newly Democratizing States," *Social Science Quarterly,* March.

Goldstein, Elizabeth and Jan Vanous, (1983), "Country Risk Analysis: Pitfalls of Comparing the Eastern Bloc Countries with the Rest of the World," *Columbia Journal of World Business*, Winter.

Gonzalez, Manolete V. and Edwin B. Villanuova, (1992), "Steering a Subsidiary Through a Political Crisis," *Risk Management,* October.

Gregory, Ann, (1988), "Integrative and Protective Techniques in Reducing Political Risk: A Comparison of American and Canadian firms in Indonesia," in Jerry Rogers, Ed., *Global Risk Assessments: Issues, Concepts, and Applications*, Book 3, Riverside, CA: GRA, Inc.,

Grosse, Robert and John Stack, (1984), "Non-economic Risk Evaluation in Multinational Banks," *Management International Review*, Vol. 24.

Hadjikani, Amjad, (1998), "Political Risk for Project-Selling Firms: Turbulence in Relationships Between Business and non-business Actors," *Journal of Business & Industrial Marketing,* Vol. 13.

Hampton, John, (1991), "Managing Risks in Chinese Joint Ventures," *Risk Management,* April.

Hare, Dean O., (1994), "Target: CEO," *Risk Management,* Vol. 41.

Harvey, Michael G., (1993), "A Survey of Corporate Programs for Managing Terrorist Threats," *Journal of International Business Studies*, Vol. 24.

_____, (1985) "A New Corporate Weapon Against Terrorism, *Business Horizons*, Vol. 28.

_____, (1981), "The Vanishing Multinational Marketing Executives: Protecting Them Against Terrorists, The Changing Marketing Environment: New Theories and Applications, *Proceedings of the American Marketing Association,* August.

_____, (1983), "Violence For Effect: Terrorist vs. MNCs, *Public Relations Journal,* October.

_____, and C. Patton, (1982), "Executive Protection Against Terrorists: Is the Best Defense a Good Offence?" *Proceedings, Academy of International Business,* December.

Hashmi, M. Anaam and Turgut Guvenli, (1992), "Importance of Political Risk Assessment Function in U.S. Multinational Corporations," *Global Finance Journal,* Vol. 3.

Heaney, Richard, and Vince Hooper, (1999), "World, Regional, and Political Risk Influences upon Asia Pacific Equity Market Returns," *Australian Journal of Management*, December.

Herrick, R. C., (1997), "Exploring the Efficient Frontier: Global Risk Management Strategies," *Risk Management,* August.

Hershberger, Robert A., (1979), "International Risk Management: Some Peculiar Considerations," *Risk Management*, Vol. 23.

Hirsh, Michael, (1993), "Have Political-Risk Analysts Got Asia's Number?" *Institutional Investor*, May.

_____, (1993), "Can You Really Quantify Political Risk?" *Institutional Investor*, April.

Hoekman, Bernard, (1997), "Competition Policy and the Global Trading System," *The World Economy,* July 1997.

Howard, Lisa, (2000), "RMs Need to Assess Cross-Border Risks," *National Underwriter/Property & Casualty Risks & Benefits*, May.

Howell, Llewellyn D., (1992), "Political Risk and Political Loss for Foreign Investment," *The International Executive*, November/December.

_____, (1986), "Area Specialists and Expert Data: The Human Factor in Political Risk Analysis," in Jerry Rogers, ed., *Global Risk Assessments: Issues, Concepts & Applications*, Book 2, Riverside, CA: GRA, Inc.

_____, (2000), "The Hard Facts of Political Risk in Emerging Markets," *Financial Planner*, December.

_____, (1997), "Forecasting Political Risk," in the *Blackwell Encyclopedia of International Management*, Cambridge, MA: Blackwell Publishers.

_____, (1998), "Keene Industries in Liberia: A Political Risk Case Study and Teaching Note," in *International Studies Notes*, Spring.

_____, (1997), "Operationalizing Political Risk in International Business: The Concept of a Politically-based Loss," in Jerry Rogers, ed., *Global Risk Assessments*, Book 4, Riverside, CA: GRA Inc.

_____, (2000), "Political Risk in Southeast Asia: From Theory to Practice," *Journal of Diplomacy and Foreign Relations*, June.

_____, (1994), "Socio-Political Risk and Its Impact on Foreign Direct Investment," *STRATEGI: Journal of Strategic Studies and International Relations*, (Malaysia Armed Forces Defence College), February.

_____ and Donald Xie, (1996), "Asia at Risk: The Impact of Methodology in Forecasting," *Management Decision*, November.

_____, and Brad Chaddick, (1994), "Models of Political Risk for Foreign Investment and Trade: An Assessment of Three Approaches," *Columbia Journal of World Business*, Fall.

_____, Syed Rizvi and Chris Cogswell, (1993), "Political Risk in Southeast Asia: A Perspective Through the Economist Model," *Journal of Asian Business*, Spring.

_____, Pola Singh and Teo Suat Cheng, (1989), "Systematic Political Risk Analysis," *INTAN Journal* (Malaysia) September.

Humphrey, Peter, (2000), "To Avoid Common Pitfall, Look before You Leap," *The China Business Review*, January/February.

Ingam, Aliya, (2000), "Risky Business," *Global Finance*, February.

Jedrzej, Frynas, (1998), "Political Instability and Business: Focus on Shell in Nigeria," *Third World Quarterly,* Vol. 19..

Joelson, Daniel, (1999), "Risky Business: Perils of Latin American Securitization," *Global Finance*, November.

Johnston, Felton McL., (1984), "Political Risk Market Expansion Broadens OPIC's Role," *Risk Management*, February.

Joung, J. K., (2000), "China's Political Risk," *Pensions and Investments*, February.

Kaminski, Bartlomiej, (1989), "International Finance and East-West Relations," *Journal of Business and Economic Perspectives*, Fall..

Kassicieh, S.K. and J.R. Nasser, (1982), "Political Risk and the Multinational Corporation: A Study of the Impact of the Iranian Revolution on Saudi Arabia, Kuwait, and the United Arab Emirates," *Management International Review*, July.

_____, (1988), "Political risk in the Gulf: the impact of the Iran Iraq War on governments and multinational corporations," *California Management Review*, Winter.

Kelly, William P., (1983), "Two Different Worlds: Corporate and Academic Techniques," *Theory and Practice in Political Risk Analysis*, Princeton University.

Kennedy, Charles R. Jr., (1992), "Relations between Transitional Corporations and Governments of Host Countries: A Look to the Future," *Transnational Corporations*, February.

Kennedy, John Whitcomb, (1984), "Risk Assessment for the U.S. Affiliates Based in Less Developed Countries," *The Columbia Journal of World Business*, Summer.

Kielmas, Maria, (1999) "Political Risks Emerge As Global Landscape Changes Managing Risks of Doing Business Internationally Requires Knowledge of Cultures, Infrastructure," Special Report, p. G2 (1999), Crain Communications, Inc. *Business Insurance*, June.

_____, (1998), "Cover for Iran Trade Resumes: European Agencies End Hiatus on Political Risk Coverage for Iran," *Business Insurance*, August.

Kobrin, Stephen J., (1978), "When Does Political Instability Result in Increased Investment Risk?," *The Columbia Journal of World Business*, Fall.

_____, (1978), "Political Risk: A Review and Reconsideration," *Journal of International Business Studies*, October.

Konrad, Kai A., Trond E. Olsen, and Ronnie Schob, (1994), "Resource Extraction and the Threat of Possible Expropriation: The Role of Swiss Bank Accounts," *Journal of Environmental Economics and Management,* March.

Kouyoumdjian, Armen, (1984), "Integrating Political and Economic Analysis-New Techniques," in *Theory and Practice of Political Risk Analysis*, University of Texas.

Kovanda, Karel, (1984), "Characteristics of the Ideal Political Risk Analysts," in *Theory and Practice of Political Risk Analysis*, University of Texas.

Kramer, Robert D., (1981) "Political Risk Assessment: A Brief Review of the State of the Art," *New International Realities*, August.

Kurland, Orin M., (1992), "Emerging Risks in Latin America," *Risk Management,* April.

Lambert, Caroline, "(2000), Political Risk Insurance Planned by COMESA," *African Business*, April.

Landon, Thomas, (1991), "Capacity to Pay: A New Debt Negotiating Strategy?" *SAIS Review*, Summer/Fall.

Laney, Leroy O., (1987), "The Secondary Market in Developing Country Debt: Some Observations and Policy Implications," *Federal Reserve Bank of Dallas Economic Review*, July.

Lau, Siu-Kai, (1992), "Social Irrelevance of Politics: Hong Kong Chinese Attitude Toward Political Leadership," *Pacific Affairs,* Summer.

Laurie, Donald L., (1982), "International Risk: Six Questions for the Concerned Executive," *Planning Review*, November.

Lawson, James C., "(1989), Political Risk Gets Riskier," *Institutional Investor*, October.

Loavy, Brian, (1984), "Assessing Country Risk for Foreign Investment Decisions," *Long Range Planning,* Vol. 17.

Lensink, Robert, (2000), "Capital Flight and Political Risk," *Journal of International Money and Finance,* February.

Lent, Ron, (1998), "Political Risk Buyers Find No Shortage In US: Middle-Size Firms Want The Coverage As They Expand Around The Globe," *Journal of Commerce,* July.

Lenway, Stefanie Ann, and Beverly Crawford, (1986), "When Business Becomes Politics: Risk and Uncertainty in East West Trade," *In Research,*

Lucero, Robert, (1993), "Businesses Can Reduce Riot Risks," *Risk Management*, March.

Madison, Christopher, (1985), "Kissinger Firm Hopes to Make Its Mark as Risk Advisors to Corporate Chiefs," *National Journal*, June.

Madrid, Raul L., (1990). "Overexposed: U.S. Banks Confront the Third World Debt Crisis," *Investor Responsibility Research Center.*

Mahoney, P.F., (1992), "Protecting Overseas Operations," *Risk Management*, October.

Majhija, Mona Verma, (1993), "Government Intervention in the Venezuelan Petroleum Industry: An Empirical Investigation of Political Risk," *Journal of International Business Studies,* Vol. 24.

Mandel, Robert, (1988), "Predicting Overseas Political Instability: Perspectives of the Government Intelligence and Multinational Business Communities," *Conflict Quarterly*, Spring.

_____, (1984), "The Overseas Private Investment Corporation and International Investment," *Columbia Journal of World Business*, Spring.

Marcus, Alfred A. and Baruch Mevorach, (1988), "Planning for the U.S. Political Cycle," *Long Range Planning*, August.

Marks, Siegfried, (1984), "Country Risk Analysis: Information Collection-Principles and Problems," in *Theory and Practice in Political Risk Analysis*, University of Texas.

Markwick, Sandy, (1996), "The Outlook for Global Risk in 1997," *Risk Management*, November.

Martinson, Michael G., and James V. Houpt, (1989), "Transfer Risk in US Banks," *Federal Reserve Bulletin*, April.

Maxwell, Charles E. and Lawrence J. Gitman, (1989), "Risk Transmission in International Banking: An Analysis of 48 Central Banks," *Journal of International Business Studies*, Summer.

_____, (1998), "Trends in Political Risk for Corporate Investors," in T. Moran, ed., *Managing International Political Risk.*

McClenahan, John S., (1989), "Aboard the Orient Distress," *Industry Week*, October.

_____, (1991), "Measuring Regional Risk," *América Economía*, Special Issue, December.

Meldrum, Duncan H., (2000), "Country Risk and Foreign Direct Investment," *Business Economics*, January.

_____, (1999), "Country Risk and a Quick Look at Latin America, *Business Economics*, July.

Mehta, Vikram S., (1993), "Political Risk: An Oil Company's Perspective," *Theory and Practice in Political Risk Analysis*, Princeton University.

Merrill, James, (1982), "Country Risk Analysis," *Columbia Journal of World Business,* Spring.

Miccolis, Jerry, and Timothy P. Quinn, (1996), "What's Your Appetite for Risk?" *Risk Management,* November.

Mitchell, Thomas H., (1984), "Corporate Security in an Age of Terrorism," *The Canadian Business Review*, Spring.

Mobius, Mark J., (1995/1996), "Risks and Rewards: Explaining Investments in Emerging Markets," *Harvard Business Review*, Winter.

Moore, Howard, (1999), "Hedging Political Risk," *Global Finance,* September.

Munpower, Jerly L., et.al., (1987), "Expert Judgments of Political Riskiness," *Journal of Forecasting*, January/March.

O'Hare, Dean, (1994), "Target: Ceo in Global Terms Kidnap and Ransom is on the Rise," *risk Management,*" July.

O'Leary, Christopher, (1999), "Mexican political Risk-Insured Deal May Spawn a Trend," *Investment Dealer's Digest,* November.

Pahl, Teresa, (1997), "Emerging Issues in Global Risk Management," *Risk Management,* February.

Paradine, Terry J., (1996), "Venturing Abroad: The Challenges of Emerging Economies," *Risk Management*, July.

Pelland, David, (1997), "Demand Grows for Political Risk Coverage: Seeking International Protection," *Risk Management*, August.

Phillips-Patrick, Frederick J., (1991), "Political Risk and Organizational Form," *Journal of Law & Economics,* October.

Piggot, C., and F. Salmon, (1996), "The Past Three Years," *Euromoney,* May.

Piturro, Marlene, (1988), "Southeast Asia: Doing Business in Paradise?" *Management Review,* July.

Poirier, Robert A. and Stephen Wright, (1990), "North-South Relations and Political Risk Analysis," *International Third World Studies Journal and Review,* Vol. 2.

Powell, Andrew, (1989), "The Management of Risk in Developing Country Finance," *Oxford Review of Economic Policy*, Winter.

_____, (1982), "Government Intervention in Less Developed Countries: the Experience of Multinational Companies," *Journal of International Business Studies*, Vol. 13.

Ptaszynski, Joseph, (2000), "Foreign Exposure for Global Property," *Risk Management*, May.

Raddock, David M., (1986), "Political Risk: Some Salient Questions," *Global Risk Assessments: Issues, Concepts, and Applications*, Jerry Rogers, ed., GRA, Inc., Riverside, CA.

Radetzki, Marian, (1982), "Has Political Risk Scared Mineral Investment Away from the Deposits in Developing Countries?," *World Development*, January.

Rarick, Charles A., (2000), "Determinants and Assessment of Political Risk in Central America," *S.A.M. Advanced Management Journal*, Summer.

Rayfield, Gordon, (1983), "Comparative Politics Applied: Theory and Practice in the Business Environment," in *Theory and Practice in Political Risk Analysis*, Princeton University.

Revzan, Henry, (1984), "Risk Management Implications," *Management Review*, April.

Rice, Gillian, and Essam Mahmoud, (1986), "A Managerial Procedure for Political Risk Forecasting," *Management International Review*, Vol. 26.

_____, (1990), "Political Risk Forecasting by Canadian Firms," *International Journal of Forecasting,"* Vol. 6.

Richardson, Helen L., (1999), "Global Risk Factors: Politics & Economics," *Transportation & Distribution*, June.

Rivard, Richard J. and Khanh Hoang Ta, (2000), "Investing in Vietnam," *Business and Economic Review,* January/March.

Robock, S.H., (1971), "Political Risk: Identification and Assessment," *Columbia Journal of World Business*, July/August.

Rogers, Jerry, (1992), "Political Risk Analysis: State of the Art 1989," *Risk Management Review*, Spring.

_____ and Richard S. Karplus, (1983), "Political Risk Analysis: The Foresight Dimension," in *Theory and Practice in Political Risk Analysis*, Princeton University.

Romano, Gerry, (1998), "Hong Kong and China: Worth the Risk?" *Association Management,* August.

Rummel, Rudolf and David Heenan, (1978), "How Multinationals Analyze Political Risk," *Harvard Business Review*, January-February.

Sacks, Paul and Stephen Blank, (1981), "Forecasting Political Risk," *Corporate Director*, September/October.

Sauers, Daniel, (1992), "A Strategic Approach to Political Risk Assessment," *Journal of Business Strategies*, Spring.

Schmidt, David A., (1986), "Analyzing Political Risk," *Business Horizons,* July/August.

Schollhammer, Hans and Douglas Nigh, (1984), "The Effect of Political Events on Foreign Direct Investments by German Multinational Corporations," *Management International Review*, Vol. 24.

Scott, Bruce R., (1984), "Country Analysis," *Harvard Business Review*, March.

Sekely, William S. and J. Markham Collins, (1988), "Cultural Influences on International Capital Structure," *Journal of International Business Studies,* Vol. 19, No. 4.

Sethi, S. Prakash and K.A.N. Luther, (1986), "Political Risk Analysis and Direct Foreign Investment: Some Problems of Definition and Measurement," *California Management Review*, Winter.

Settembrino, François, (1994), "Risk Management in Enterprise: A Systematic Approach," *Risk Management*, August.

Shapiro, Alan C., (1981), "Managing Political Risk: A Policy Approach," *Columbia Journal of World Business*, Fall.

Shapiro, Harvey, "(1996), Know Your Local Candidates," *Infrastructure Finance,* October.

_____, (1997), "A Less Dismal Science?" *Institutional Investor,* Vol. 22.

Shreeve, Thomas W., (1984), "Be Prepared for Political Changes Abroad," *Harvard Business Review*, July/August.

Sikes, Jonathan, (1989), "Vietnam Welcomes the Oil Companies but It Could Be Risky," *Energy Economist: an International Analysis,* October.

Simon, Denis Fred, (1990), "After Tiananmen: What is the future for foreign business in China?," *California Management Review*, Winter.

Simon, Jeffrey D., (1982), "Political Risk Assessment: Past Trends and Future Prospects," *Columbia Journal of World Business*, Fall.

_____, (1985), "Political Risk Forecasting," *Futures: The Journal of Forecasting and Planning*, April.

_____, (1984), "A Theoretical Perspective on Political Risk," *Journal of International Business Studies,* Winter.

Sloan, Michael P., (1984), "Strategic Planning by Multiple Political Futures Techniques," *Management International Review*, Vol. 24.

Snider, Lewis W., (1986), "Political Capacity and Political Risk: the Development and Validation of a Measure," *Global Risk Assessments: Issues, Concepts and Applications*, ed. Jerry Rogers, GRA, Inc. Riverside, CA.

Stern, Richard, (1982), "Insurance for Third World Currency Inconvertibility Protection," *Harvard Business Review*, (May/June 1982.

Stevens, Flumo Y., (1997), "Quantitative Perspective on Political Risk Analysis for Direct Foreign Investment- a Closer Look," *Multinational Business Review*, Spring.

Subramanian, R., Motwani, J. and Ishak, S., (1993), "Political Risk Analysis of U.S. Firms: A Theoretical Framework and an Empirical Analysis," *Multinational Business Review*, Fall.

Sweeney, Paul, (1999). "The World Bank Battles the Cancer of Corruption," *Global Finance,* October.

Tarzi, Shaw M., (1997), "Country Risk Analysis, International Banking and the Developing Countries," *The Journal of Social, Political and Economic Studies,* Winter.

Thorndike, Tony, (1992), "Prediction and Forecasting: The Contrasting Fortunes of International Relations and Political Risk Analysis," *Risk Management Review,* Spring.

Torre, Jose de la, and David H. Neckar, (1988), "Forecasting Political Risks for International Operations," *International Journal of Forecasting.*

Tullis, Melissa and Oliver Bouin, (1990), "Investment Prospects in Eastern Europe," *Multinational Business*, Summer.

Turner, Bill, (1992), "Political Risk Management in Mining Investment Decisions," *The Practicing Manager*, October.

Vernon, Raymond, (1980), "The Obsolescing Bargain: A Key Factor in Political Risk," *The International Essays for Business Decision Makers*, Vol. 5, Mark B. Winchester, ed., Houston, Texas: Center for International Business.

Wagner, Daniel, (1999), "The Cluster Trend: Political Risk, Part II," *Risk Management*, September.

_____, (1994), "A New World for Political Risk Investment Insurance," *Risk Management*, October.

_____, (1997), "The Resurgence of Political Risk," *Risk Management*, November.

_____, (1991), "Transition in Eastern Europe: The Case for Political Risk Insurance," *The East/West Business Report*, April.

_____, (1990), "Why Political Risk Insurance Will Grow in the 1990's," *Risk Management*, October.

Walder, Andrew G., (1991), "Workers, Managers, and the State: The Reform Era and the Political Crisis," *The China Quarterly,* September.

Wallace, Laura, (1992), "MIGA: Up and Running," *Finance & Development*, March.

Walther, James R., and Debra M. Van Alstyne, (1984), "Mergers and Acquisitions: A How-To Perspective…," *Management Review*, April.

Wand, Shou Qing, Robert L.K. Tiong, Seng Kiong Ting and David Ashley, (1999), "Political Risks: Analysis of Key Contract Clauses in China's BOT Project," *Journal of Construction Engineering and Management*, May/June.

Weigel, Dale R., (1988), "Investment in LDCs: the Debate Continues," *The Columbia Journal of World Business*, Spring.

Weiner, Benjamin, (1992), "What Executives Should Know About Political Risk," *Management Review*, January.

West, Gerald T., (1996), "Managing Project Political Risk: The Role of Investment Insurance," *The Journal of Project Finance*, Winter.

Wilkin, Sam, (2000), "Why Political Risk is Important to You," *World Trade*, March.

Willyard, Jack, and Peter Rodaway, (1992), "Protection in a Volatile World," *Excess and Surplus Lines*, February.

Wilson, Robert, (1992), "Managing Political Risk," *Institutional Investor*, November.

Young, Kitty Y., (1993), "Political Risk Under ' One Country Two Systems': A Conjoint Analysis," *Journal of Asian Business*, Winter.

Zloch-Christy, Iliana, (1989), "East European Creditworthiness: Problems of Country Risk Analysis," *Osteuropa Wirtschaft*, June.